REA

ACPL ITEM
DISCARDED

362.1 C16R
CANHAM-CLYNE, JOHN.
THE RATIONAL OPTION

The

FOR A NATIONAL

Rational

HEALTH PROGRAM

Option

The Rational Option

FOR A NATIONAL

HEALTH PROGRAM

Option

By **John Canham-Clyne**
with **Steffie Woolhandler, M.D.**
and **David Himmelstein, M.D.**

THE PAMPHLETEER'S PRESS, INC., STONY CREEK, CONNECTICUT

Allen County Public Library
900 Webster Street
PO Box 2270
Fort Wayne, IN 46801-2270

Copyright © *John Canham-Clyne, David Himmelstein,
and Steffie Woolhandler, 1995.*

COVER AND BOOK DESIGN BY BARBARA MARKS

All rights reserved

Library of Congress Catalog Card Number 94-074595

ISBN 0-9630587-1-1 (Paperback)   0-9630587-2-X (Hardcover)

*THE PAMPHLETEER'S PRESS
P.O. Box 3374, Stony Creek, Connecticut 06405
Tel/Fax: 203-483-1429*

A Note of Thanks

Every book is to some degree a collaboration. As the title page suggests, this one is more so than most. It began with Larry Lifschultz and Rabia Ali's vision of bringing the work of leading academics to bear on pressing public issues in an accessible form. The book would never have seen the light of day without the long hours Larry and Rabia labored over the manuscript. Steffie Woolhandler, David Himmelstein, and their colleagues laid the foundation for this work through years of rigorous research and vigorous activism. Throughout the creation of *The Rational Option,* David and Steffie infused the project with their intellectual power and giving spirit. It is a privilege to share authorship with them.

Joanne Landy gave generously of her time reading the manuscript, suggested changes during the editing process, and dealt James Madison a fatal blow along the way. Dr. Marvin Zimmerman offered detailed comments which rightfully insisted on greater precision at several key points. James Mooney of the Yale University Press applied a meticulous copyeditor's pen. Karen Suchenski proofread the text with a careful and professional eye. Thanks are due to Ellen Shaffer in Senator Paul Wellstone's office for coordinating the introduction. Melissa Canham-Clyne bore with good humor my anguish at Larry's invariably ill-timed requests for yet another addition or revision.

The chapter on long-term care is a truncated version of the Physicians for a National Health Program's proposal for a long-term care system, and my only role was to reduce the length of the text. The proposal was drafted by PNHP's Working Group on Long-Term Care Program Design: Charlene Harrington, R.N., Ph.D., Christine Cassel, M.D., Carroll L. Estes, Ph.D., Steffie Woolhandler, M.D., M.P.H., David Himmelstein, M.D., William H. Barker, M.D., Kenneth R. Barney, M.D., Thomas Bodenheimer, M.D., David Carrell, Ph.D., Lewanda Cox, Kenneth B. Frisof, M.D., Judith B. Kaplan, M.S., Peter D. Mott, M.D., Robert J. Newcomer, Ph.D., David C. Parish, M.D., M.P.H., James H. Sanders, Jr., M.D., Lillian Rabinowitz, and Howard Waitzkin, M.D., Ph.D..

Finally, this book would not be worth writing if there were not millions of Americans tirelessly organizing to bring about an inclusive, caring health care system in the United States. *The Rational Option* is dedicated to the consumer advocates, labor activists, peace and justice workers, religious groups, health care professionals, legislators, patients and citizens working to bring about a single-payer system. If it persuades just one of their neighbors or colleagues, it will have been worth the effort because this battle can only be won at the grass roots, one citizen at a time.

JOHN CANHAM-CLYNE
Arlington, Virginia

Contents

GRAPHS

The

FOR A NATIONAL

Rational

HEALTH PROGRAM

Option

3 1833 02664 1495

Introduction

By Senator Paul Wellstone

The ultimate irony for single-payer advocates must be that every proposal for national health care reform died in Congress because none was politically feasible. As the authors of this volume demonstrate convincingly, the single-payer proposal is the most rational policy solution to the unique crises of the U. S. health care system: skyrocketing costs coupled with plummeting access to care. It is simple, straightforward, effective, and remarkably successful in other countries. The American Health Security Act (S. 491/H.R. 1200), a single-payer proposal, which we introduced in the Senate and the House in March 1993, was rated by the Congressional Budget Office as most effective in saving money, and therefore capable of covering every American with a comprehensive range of benefits.

The special interests inside the Washington Beltway immediately went to work discrediting our proposal. It was not politically feasible, they said. From the point of view of the health insurance industry and certain other health care companies, that was a wish as much as a prediction. A single-payer approach would streamline the bloated administrative bureaucracy that eats up over 10 percent of our trillion dollar health care budget every year and could also reduce the role of insurance companies. But the public remained curious. With the active support of advocates around the country, we kept the single-payer alternative alive throughout the two-year Congressional debate on health care reform.

For years to come politicians and analysts will debate what went wrong. As we look back on the failure of the 103rd Congress to pass any health care reform, and ahead to the future, some clear ideas emerge. President Clinton and Hillary Rodham Clinton deserve tremendous credit for finally bringing the health care crisis, at once a threat to our economy and a very personal concern for millions of Americans, to the forefront of the national agenda. However, this book takes careful aim at the political and policy shortcomings of their effort and their proposal. It is by now standard to point to the many months devoted to developing a complex proposal that had no strong political support, that either compromised too much or too little to begin with (depending on your point of view), and deteriorated from there. By comparing the Clintons' proposal point for point with single-payer, this book makes a valuable contribution to our analysis of a critical moment in history, as well as a primer for those who will continue the effort.

The managed competition proposal of the Clintons was supposed to mollify the health care special interests, while achieving cost control and universal coverage. It relied on unreliable allies—the health care industry and big business—and failed to ignite the imagination of consumers and activists. When the Clinton plan was faltering, why wasn't there a massive outcry for a single-payer solution from the many constituencies who had so much to gain from reform—and who now stand to lose so much more—including older Americans, union members, the uninsured and underinsured, people with disabilities, people with "pre-existing conditions," women, rural Americans, health care providers of conscience, people of color?

One reason is that there were legitimate grounds for disagreement on the merits of the Clinton plan itself. The proposal changed from week to week, depending on which interest group had exerted influence most recently, making it as difficult for consumer groups to consolidate opposition to the plan as it was ultimately difficult for the administration to consolidate support. And there were legitimate questions that advocacy groups and their leaders had to confront.

Many agreed with the authors of this book that the plan would have done little more than consolidate the power of the insurance industry and make further reform impossible, and attacked the proposal for the tremendous bureaucracy it would have had to create to mitigate the discrimination and inequality inherent in its market-oriented approach. Others could see some improvements that the bill would achieve, laying the groundwork for the ability to fight another day to overcome its undeniable shortcomings. Universal coverage, coupled with an enormous expansion of consumers' rights, the promise of cost control, and the ability of states to implement single-payer systems, could have provided that framework to hold the system accountable when it, inevitably, did not work.

The overwhelming factor, though, was the multi-million-dollar campaign to hijack reform. The very special interests the Clinton plan tried to accommodate joined forces with corporate America to perpetrate the most heavily financed and most misleading campaign of opposition seen to date in Congress. A publicity war of fear-mongering and confusion hit the public in its most vulnerable spot—mistrust of government—and millions of dollars in contributions to members of Congress by special interest lobbyists reinforced the point: don't mess with the status quo.

Well-organized forces of the medical-industrial complex, including insurers, drug makers, HMOs, medical trade associations, health care providers, and similar groups, killed reform efforts by pouring money into Congressional campaign coffers at an unprecedented rate. The evidence, although circumstantial, is overwhelming: coupled with massive ad campaigns for which these groups paid over $50 million, their contributions had a devastating effect on the health care policy process. Americans—even those with good health care—will pay a terrible price for this failure, and health care costs will continue to rise dramatically.

The collapse of health care reform underscores the critical need to enact immediately the campaign finance legislation that was killed by a Republican-led Senate filibuster, even in the face of a House–Senate agreement to lower PAC contributions. These huge amounts of money distort our process of representative government. To many, we don't have representative democracy, we have auction-block democracy.

Citizen Action, the nation's largest consumer organization, studied Federal Election Commission records and reported that from January 1993 through July 1994, political contributions to Members of Congress from health reform opponents stood at over $46 million—most targeted to key Congressional health care committees. That industry contributions are targeted so intensively to these committees—and would be, regardless of the ideology, region, or party of their members—belies arguments that contributions are not made to further policy agendas. This time, reform opponents invested in a policy outcome favorable to them: inaction. Their investment paid off.

This is not the first time that health care special interests have killed reform. Since just before World War I, when reformers pressed for national health insurance as similar programs were being put in place in Western Europe, powerful lobbies have opposed it. From the 1930s through the 1980s, driven largely by the grassroots demands of Americans without health care, comprehensive reform seemed an idea whose time had come, and come, and come again. But each time, reform was hijacked by industry interests—to the detriment of millions of Americans with little or no care.

The insurance industry lobby, formed to spearhead opposition to reform, provides a good example of the tactics of special interests, and of the relationship between political contributions and influence. In their lobbying packet, according to an industry newsletter, the group urged its allies in each state to review Federal Election Commission reports to identify large contributors to key Senators and Representatives, and then arrange meetings between their contributor allies and members from that state, in order to make their case against reform. Not very subtle, but it gets the job done.

The single-payer proposal actually outlived the Clinton proposal's relatively brief life in Congress. The House Education and Labor Committee passed the American Health Security Act intact, while also approving a version of the Clinton bill. As the Committee process wore on, it became clear that the millions spent had not been in vain. As Republicans began to sniff electoral victory at the polls, they were joined by conservative Democrats in assuring what had been unthinkable as recently as the spring of 1994: that no reform bill would pass. Republican filibusters halted debate on even the most hobbled proposal before the Senate, giving birth to an even more distorted effort that declared itself the "mainstream" proposal—despite the fact that it evoked nearly unanimous opposition from consumer and provider organizations, from unions to religiously based hospitals.

The legacy for single-payer supporters is mixed. The crisis can only deepen, as more people lose coverage and as the industry, emboldened by the failure of reform, once again sets about inflating charges at an uncontrolled rate. More people have become educated about a single-payer system, and an initiative on the California ballot for November 1994 built a significant grassroots network.

But real progress requires a long-range view. The conventional wisdom now would suggest that the Clinton proposal failed because it was not sufficiently bipartisan, and is now defining the "mainstream" proposal as a starting point for political feasibility. An unmitigated disaster, this latter proposal would strip away benefits and rights that many insured Americans now enjoy, dismantle Medicaid—the program that finances health care for the poor—leaving poor people at the mercy of corporatized, private sector health care, and slash the Medicare program for the elderly and disabled. It would do little if anything to expand access, and has no pretense of being able to control costs.

At the same time, a counter-revolution is underway on the ground floor of the health care delivery system. The forces of competition unleashed by the very unveiling of the Clinton plan are achieving many of the plans objectives, without the legislation. Large corporate health plans and insurance companies are merging at an unprecedented rate, while corporations themselves are deciding that they are the best candidates to run health plans for their employees through "self-funded" plans accountable to no one. The result is that many Americans are losing any choice they may have had of doctors and other health care providers, the quality of care is giving way to concerns for the bottom line, and cost increases continue to be shifted with impunity from employers to employees. As a few large insurance companies come to dominate the managed care marketplace, accountability to consumers and providers is flying out the window. Price increases, temporarily constrained by the threat of reform, are likely to ensue.

The American health care system cannot continue forever consuming an ever larger share of gross national product—now at 15 percent—while the number of people with insurance falls and the seven minute doctor visit becomes the standard. It is up to us and the other advocates for a rational, single-payer solution to our health care crisis to join the authors of this book in spreading the word, and to build support among the majority of Americans who will join us if we can reach them.

Washington, D.C.

The Rational Option

The current health care reform debate is distinguished by denials of our problems and an isolationist sentiment that refuses to learn from other countries and other times. One of the enduring clichés of this health care debate is that the United States has the "the best health care system in the world." It is a claim that Senator Robert Dole and the Republican party have made frequently.[1] Yet among industrialized nations the United States alone has failed to deliver basic medical care to all of its people while spending far more money on health care than any other society. Policy makers in the United States today face a distinctly American failure.

Almost a quarter century ago the United States stood astride the globe as an unrivaled economic superpower. It was routine then to describe the United States as the wealthiest society in history. Although its economy had been growing steadily since the 1950s, Germany's landscape still bore the deep scars from World War II. France, similarly damaged by two World Wars, could barely be described as a major industrial power. Great Britain, newly bereft of empire, watched its standard of living slowly decline. Nonetheless, nearly all of the devastated states that emerged from World War II today have populations in better health than ours. The United States ranks twenty-first among the twenty-four largest industrial nations in infant mortality, and sixteenth worldwide in life expectancy, yet spends more than 40 percent more per capita on health care than any other nation.[2]

Choked with bureaucracy, outrageously expensive, often indifferent to suffering, the American health care system delivers too much of the wrong kind of care to patients who can pay, and refuses essential services to those who cannot. Virtually every American counts among family, friends, or coworkers someone who has been mistreated by the medical system.

More and more Americans who think of themselves as middle class—both employed and insured—find their coverage eroding. Many corporate employers have suddenly terminated benefits that they had guaranteed for decades. For example, McDonnell-Douglas West, Primerica Corporation and several other large companies recently reneged on promised health care benefits for retirees. In March 1993, the Senate Labor and Human Resources Committee received testimony from Casey Patelski, a recent McDonnell-Douglas retiree. Under contract from NASA, Patelski acted as "mission control" for the moon landings. Suffering from polio, Patelski will find it impossible to purchase private insurance. Nevertheless, McDonnell-Douglas West, citing new accounting regulations, informed Patelski and more than three thousand other retirees that the company will stop funding their health benefits.[3]

For the thirty-nine million Americans who lack insurance altogether, or the tens of millions more with only partial coverage, the situation is also grim.[4] Nearly three hundred thousand Americans are refused care each year at hospital Emergency Departments because they are uninsured or inadequately insured.[5] The National Medical Expenditure Survey found that in 1987 nearly one-half million Americans tried but failed to get emergency care because they had a negative "wallet biopsy," inadequate medical insurance.[6] Low-income patients who manage to scrape together the money to see a doctor often cannot afford the medications and therapies their physicians prescribe.

This distinctly American tragedy results from deliberate policy choices made by successive congresses and presidents in the thrall of powerful vested interests. It is a situation which can be altered. But universal and affordable coverage will only be achieved if an aroused public demands it from their elected representatives.

The United States has approached a crossroads where an opportunity has arisen to extend the definition of citizenship. A successful reform of the U.S. health care system can result in a lasting contribution to the country's domestic tranquillity and general welfare. By improving the standard of living and health

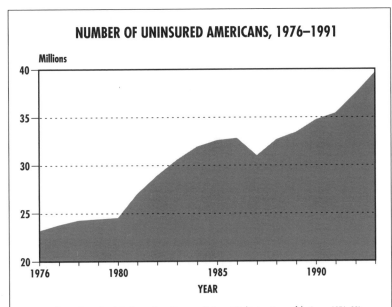

NUMBER OF UNINSURED AMERICANS, 1976–1991

Source: *Current Population Survey: Annual Demographic Report* (Washington: Bureau of the Census, 1976–90)

In 1991 more people were uninsured than at any time since the passage of Medicare and Medicaid in the mid-1960s. The number of uninsured increased by two million between 1989 and 1991 following a rise of 700,000 between 1988 and 1989. By 1991 at least eleven million more people were uninsured than in 1980. On the basis of these trends, the Employee Benefit Research Institute in Washington projects that in 1994 there were forty-one million people uninsured in the United States.

of the American people a significant social advance will have been accomplished. The accelerating collapse of U.S. health care requires a fundamental overhaul. Only a basic restructuring of the American health care system can address the crisis. But what kind of restructuring?

In his September 1993 speech to Congress announcing his reform proposal, Bill Clinton set lofty goals for health care reform: universal coverage, cost savings, simplicity, choice, quality. Clinton summed up the problems facing the American people: "On any given day more than 38.9 million Americans, most of them working people and their little children, have no health insurance at all. And in spite of all this our medical bills are growing at over twice the rate of inflation."[7] Instead of proposing a system successfully functioning well elsewhere, Clinton proposed a private insurer-based system that would perpetuate the inequality and inefficiency of American health care.

By erecting financial barriers to care, Clinton's proposal betrayed its promise of universal coverage. Because it expanded the power and dominance of the largest private insurance companies, the Clinton plan took no account of the enormous savings possible through the elimination of the insurance industry's redundant billing and payment bureaucracies. By relying on the unproved theories of "managed competition" for cost control, the Clinton proposals offered little hope of halting the inflationary health cost spiral, and would interpose more bureaucrats between doctors and their patients.

But if Clinton had looked north he would have found that our neighbors have solved the worst problems facing American medicine. The Canadian system is not perfect—no system is— yet all Canadians have insurance, they are free to choose their own doctors, and they spend only two-thirds of what we do on health care. The Canadian approach is simple and straightforward: include everyone in a single public insurance program like Social Security, cover all needed care without co-payments or deductibles, and leave patients free to choose any doctor, clinic, or hospital. Since Canada started its program twenty-five years ago, life expectancy has soared, and is now two years longer than in the United States. Canadians pay 40 percent less per person for care than Americans, but get more care, more doctor visits, more hospital care, and even more bone marrow transplants.[8] Switching to a Canadian-style single-payer system is the only solution that can meet the Clintons' professed goals of extending comprehensive health care coverage to all Americans, stopping the runaway cost increases of the current system, and allowing Americans a free choice of providers.

WHAT IS A SINGLE-PAYER SYSTEM?

The phrase "single-payer" means that one institution alone—the government—pays the nation's health care bills. Currently, doctors and hospitals are paid by private insurance companies, employers who self insure (i.e., act as their own insurers), government programs including Medicaid and Medicare, and directly by patients. Switching to a single-payer system means simplifying health insurance.

Canada, Great Britain, and several other countries have single-payer health care systems. There is an important distinction, however, between Canada's system of national health insurance, and the British National Health Service. Canadian provincial governments cover every patient with the same package of benefits, but doctors can remain in private practice and hospitals are mostly privately owned, though nonprofit. Canada has socialized insurance, not socialized medicine. Conversely, in Britain doctors receive a salary directly from the government, or a lump sum fee (capitation) for each patient who signs up with them, and government owns and operates most hospitals.

In the United States, Physicians for a National Health Program (PNHP) is a nationwide group of more than six thousand doctors founded in 1987 to promote a single-payer system modeled on the Canadian system.[9] No single piece of extant legislation adopts all of the features PNHP proposes, but the American Health Security Act, also known as the Conyers-McDermott-Wellstone bill, came closest. The House version was flawed in that it would allow for-profit HMOs to continue functioning. But each bill represented a genuine attempt to create a single-payer system.[10]

The most important feature of PNHP's proposal is the removal of all financial barriers to medical care. Every American would be covered for all necessary medical care by a public insurance plan administered by state and regional boards. Everyone would receive a card entitling him or her to standard medical care as well as mental health services, long-term care in nursing homes or at home, dental services, occupational health services, prescription drugs, and equipment. With the card, patients could visit any hospital or doctor they chose, and receive all needed medical care without deductibles, co-payments, or any out-of-pocket costs. Bills would be paid by the National Health Program.

The plan would be funded federally but administered by the states. In Canada, the provinces qualify for federal block grants by meeting the minimum specifications of universal, comprehensive coverage, portability of benefits, public administration, and no financial barriers to care. The provinces, as would the states in the United States, retain some flexibility in defining the benefit package. State health boards, either elected or appointed from the ranks of industry and consumers, would oversee the U.S. plan, set policy, and negotiate fee schedules and budgets.

Most hospitals and nursing homes would remain privately owned and operated. Their billing would be radically simplified. Instead of billing for each bandaid and aspirin tablet they would negotiate an annual "global" lump sum budget with the regional NHP board to cover all operating costs.

Capital funds for new buildings and equipment would be distributed separately by regional NHP boards on the basis of health planning goals. The current health care cost spiral is driven, in part, by a medical arms race. Private hospitals and

HMOs compete with each other for patients and physicians, with glitzy new buildings and the latest high technology equipment, whether new services are needed or not. For instance, Boston's Massachusetts General Hospital recently opened a new obstetrical service, despite being within three miles of five well-established maternity programs with surplus beds.

The impulse makes sense from the point of view of an individual hospital: a sparkling maternity suite will make the hospital attractive to insurance plans hoping to enroll affluent young families. But competition-driven hospital capital spending is dangerously inefficient. The United States already has a surplus of three hundred thousand hospital beds and at least five thousand surplus mammography machines.[11] The excess raises the cost per mammogram since most machines are used only part-time. In facilities that operate at low volumes, quality is often lower, since staff may not perform enough mammograms to maintain their competence. Uncontrolled capital spending not only raises costs, it lowers quality.

Under a single-payer system, private doctors could continue to practice on a fee-for-service basis. The regional NHP board would set simple, binding fee schedules. Nonprofit HMOs could continue receiving a yearly lump sum from the NHP for each patient to cover operating expenses, but capital would be allocated separately—a budgeting strategy that would remove most incentives to undertreat or overtreat. Neighborhood health centers, clinics, and home care agencies employing salaried doctors and other health practitioners would be funded directly from NHP on the basis of a global budget. The NHP would pay pharmacists' wholesale costs plus a reasonable dispensing fee for prescription drugs on the NHP formulary. Medical equipment would be covered in a similar fashion.

A single-payer system would prohibit private insurance for services covered by the national plan, saving at least $40 billion a year in insurance-industry profits and overhead.[12] Removing the complex and redundant insurance bureaucracy would greatly simplify paperwork for doctors and hospitals, generating billions of dollars of additional savings. More than half of the 24.8 percent of hospital budgets that now goes for billing and administration would be saved under this plan.[13]

Costs would be constrained through streamlining of billing and bureaucracy, improved health planning, and the NHP's ability to set and enforce overall spending limits. In June 1991, the U.S. General Accounting Office (GAO) found that *"[if] the United States were to shift to a system of universal coverage and a single payer, as in Canada, the savings in administrative costs would be more than enough to offset the expense of universal coverage."*[14] The PNHP proposal includes a substantial expansion of long-term care which will mean an overall increase in health care costs. However, the efficiency of a single-payer system means that additional funds will actually be spent on providing health care to those who are in need and not on bureacracy. Even with a huge boost in coverage, costs will not increase at the present astronomical rate. The Congressional Budget Office estimated that the Senate version of the American Health Security Act would save the nation $110 billion below the projected cost of the current system even *after* covering all the uninsured and dramatically improving coverage for the underinsured.[15]

Canada's government-run insurance program saves billions on bureaucracy. In Canada, health costs are around 10 percent of GNP, with 11 percent of that spent on billing and administration.[16] In the United States, health costs are 14 percent of GNP with 24 percent spent on billing and administration, even though a far lower proportion of the population receives adequate care.[17]

THE CLINTON ALTERNATIVE: MANAGED COMPETITION AND EMPLOYER MANDATES

Clinton proposed a plan that adopts two fashionable ideas for health care reform: an employer mandate and managed competition. Under the original Clinton plan's "employer mandate," all employers are required to pay 80 percent of the cost of their employees' health insurance premiums, with a system of subsidies for small businesses.

An employer mandate, by itself, may cover many Americans but will not provide universal coverage. Hawaii has a system requiring all employers to pay up to 1.5 percent of payroll for employee health insurance costs. In his address to Congress, Clinton dubbed Hawaii "the only state that covers all of their citizens and has still been able to keep costs below the national average."[18] Clinton was repeating one of the familiar myths about American health care. In a May 1993 report, Hawaii state officials claimed that all but 3.5 percent of the state's population is covered.[19]

But according to the Census Bureau's Current Population Survey, 11 percent of Hawaiians lacked insurance in 1993. Six states had less than 11 percent of their populations uninsured.[20] If Hawaii's "near-universal" coverage were extended to the whole country, more than seventeen million Americans would still lack health insurance. Thus, an employer mandate will not guarantee universal coverage.

Access to medical care continues to be a problem for many Hawaiians and, contrary to Bill Clinton's pronouncements, his own Health Care Financing Administration says that Hawaii's health costs are well above the national average. This is why three-quarters of Hawaii's congressional delegation has endorsed a single-payer system as the best solution to the nation's health care woes. Representatives Patsy Mink and Neil Abercrombie, along with Senator Daniel Inouye, were all cosponsors of the Conyers-McDermott-Wellstone single-payer bill known as the American Health Security Act, and Inouye has developed his own single-payer proposal.

It would be unfair, however, to judge the Clinton plan solely on the basis of Hawaii's failure to cover all of its citizens or to contain costs. Clinton proposed to apply the principles of "managed competition" to the American health system to control costs and expand access. The phrase "managed competition" originated in the writings of Stanford economist Alain Enthoven.[21] Enthoven further developed his ideas with a group of industry leaders who gathered periodically at the Jackson Hole, Wyoming, vacation home of physician-cum-real-estate developer Paul Ellwood. The members of the so-called Jackson Hole Group already exercise immense control in the American health care system: as executives of the nation's largest insurance firms, representatives of the pharmaceutical industry, and industry-sponsored academics.[22]

Managed competition would consolidate health care into a handful of large managed-care organizations run by large insurance companies. Insurers would be required to offer a statutory minimum package of benefits, and, theoretically, compete with one another for business. Large business would continue to purchase insurance for employees. Individuals and small businesses would join state-sponsored purchasing cooperatives, which by signing up thousands of people, would amass the same "market power" as General Motors or AT&T to bargain for lower rates from the competing plans. (The Health Insurance Purchasing Cooperatives, shortened to "HIPC," were renamed "Health Alliances" by the Clintons.) Given the quasi-monopoly that a few large plans in each region would soon attain, few expect any real competition. Rather, a few giant plans/HMOs would face off against a handful of giant employers and a Health Alliance.

Moreover, the theoretical fathers of managed competition have always seen cost control as the primary goal. Enthoven initially proposed lowering the minimum wage by eight percent so employers could afford to buy insurance for their employees.[23] The Clintons have tried to soften the rough edges surrounding the theory of managed competition by promising subsidies for small businesses and poor individuals, while maintaining the core strategy of cost control through competition. This form of competition would not lower costs, but would in fact foster control of the entire medical system by a few insurance giants.

Through the so-called Health Alliances, individuals and

small businesses would theoretically be able to choose their insurance plan. Large employers would be allowed to continue purchasing insurance in the same way they do now. According to the Clintons, each Health Alliance would offer its members a choice among several plans. "We propose," the President told Congress, "to give every American a choice among high-quality plans. You can stay with your current doctor, join a network of doctors and hospitals, or join a health maintenance organization. If you don't like your plan, every year you'll have the chance to choose a new one."[24] Yet individuals would have only the sham choice between one or another of the huge corporate HMOs with stiff financial penalties for choosing any but the cheapest plan.

Two major benefit programs that have adopted models similar to managed competition provide some insight into how it might function. Federal workers enrolled in the Federal Employee Health Benefits Program (FEHBP) may choose a new health plan each year during "open season," based on information provided by the insurers. But the FEHBP, touted by the Heritage Foundation and others as a model for managed competition, has averaged double-digit rate increases since 1984; its costs rose faster in the 1980s than overall health care costs. Furthermore, because the FEHBP fixes the government's contribution and requires employees to bear the full extra cost of better plans, a predictably multitiered system has emerged; higher-income workers have better health plans. Similarly, the California Public Employees' Retirement System (CALPERS), Alain Enthoven's favorite exemplar of managed competition, had cost increases exceeding the national average for three of the last six years. Last year CALPERS experienced no premium increases, largely due to powerful pressure from state insurance commissioner John Garamendi, whose short-term success might be viewed as a success of government regulation rather than a success of competition.

In the early 1970s, then-Governor Ronald Reagan attempted to control costs in California's Medicaid program, known as Medi-Cal, by encouraging beneficiaries to enroll in managed care plans, called Pre-paid Health Plans (PHPs). In an eerie historical echo, Reagan and state Health and Welfare Secretary Earl W. Brian, Jr. insisted that the combination of managed care and tough bargaining by the state would restrain costs.

Entrepreneurs quickly realized that the fastest route to PHP profits was to sign up healthy Medi-Cal recipients, collect their premiums, and provide little or no care. PHPs prodded the sick to drop their enrollment from the plan by refusing to answer emergency phones, delaying appointments, and encouraging physicians to prescribe tranquilizers rather than evaluate and treat illnesses.[25] Patients were so dissatisfied that two-thirds of PHP members dropped their enrollment each year and returned to the fee-for-service system, an option that will be unavailable to most patients under 1990s-style managed competition.

Moreover, the state bailed out powerful PHPs that overspent their budgets, making a mockery of cost containment. Sacramento's Foundation Community Health Plan ran up a $1.5 million deficit by March 1973. According to state law, and Reagan's cost containment theory, Foundation Community was supposed to assume the loss. But the state responded by covering the deficit, and offering an additional unsecured loan. Will modern-day regulators be more likely to let powerful insurers/HMOs fail?

The Clinton proposals would mold health plan "choices" by imposing heavy deductibles and co-payments on people who chose traditional fee-for-service plans, forcing all but the wealthy into managed care. The Clintons continue to espouse the claim that managed care will ultimately control costs. A few facts are pertinent. The expansion of HMOs in the past two decades has coincided with unprecedented cost increases. In California, more than 80 percent of all employees—including state employees covered under CALPERS—are already covered by managed care, yet costs are 19 percent above the national average and rising more rapidly.[26] Of all the fifty states, Massachusetts has both the highest proportion of its residents enrolled in HMOs and the highest per capita health care costs.

Nationwide, HMO premiums have increased at the same rate as Blue Cross premiums. Moreover, large employers and state Medicaid programs have long been engaged in the type of "hard bargaining" now envisioned under managed competition, yet their costs have continued to skyrocket.

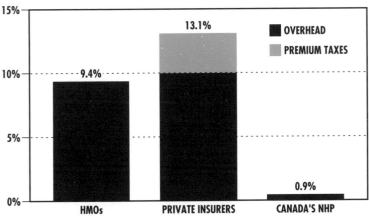

HMO EFFICIENCY? INSURANCE OVERHEAD: HMOs, PRIVATE INSURERS AND CANADA'S NHP

Source: *Source Book of Health Insurance Data* (Washington: Health Insurance Association of America, 1989);
HMO Industry Profile (Washington: Group Health Association of America, 1993)

The administrative costs of Health Maintenance Organizations (HMOs) are comparable to those of other private insurers, and far higher than those of a single-payer system. Nationwide, HMO overhead averaged 9.4 percent of total premiums in 1990, compared to the 13.1 percent overhead of other private insurance programs. However, most of this difference is accounted for by premium taxes, paid by private insurance companies, but not HMOs. The overhead costs for both HMOs and private insurance should be corrected upward for an interest credit, i.e. the money earned by investing premiums before claims are paid. Even excluding these investment earnings, both HMOs and indemnity insurers in the United States have overhead rates ten times higher than Canada's national health program.

HMO premiums are generally slightly lower than traditional insurance policies, in part because HMOs attract healthier enrollees. However, HMO costs have been rising as rapidly as traditional insurance. Even in communities with very large HMO market penetration, costs increases have continued. Hence, the theory that wide use of managed care would contain U.S. health costs has little empirical support.

This catalog of failure has been assembled mainly in urban areas, a setting where managed competition in theory is at least plausible. But in smaller cities and rural America, population is too sparse to support even a semblance of competition. A town's only HMO or hospital cannot compete with itself. Only 50 percent of Americans live in metropolitan areas populous enough to support two or three HMOs. For the rest of the nation the concept of price competition, which is so fundamental to managed competition, is inconceivable.

Moreover, managed competition will increase bureaucratic costs and waste. The Clinton proposals would replace existing government health insurance programs (which operate with relatively low administrative overheads) with more bureaucratized and wasteful private insurance. For example, the administration proposes to shift enrollees from Medicaid, a public program with administrative overhead of 5 percent to private insurance where overhead averages more than 13 percent (Canada's program runs for less than 1 percent overhead). Moreover, managed competition would add another layer of bureaucrats—the Health Alliances—who will surely join rather than replace their predecessors. Finally, tightening insurers' control of doctors and hospitals, as promised by managed competition, would increase bureaucratic burdens on doctors while placing doctors under financial pressures not to provide adequate care. The Mayo Clinic already employs seventy people just to talk on the phone with managed care utilization reviewers. Because managed competition fails to trim administrative costs (and in fact increases them), it can only expand access by increasing health spending by $70 to $90 billion annually.

Beneath managed competition's complex detail and campaign-style rhetoric lies a simple theme: keep insurance giants like Aetna and Prudential at the heart of health care. Aetna, Prudential, CIGNA, and several other insurance companies moved aggressively into managed care during the 1980s. As patients are funneled into a few plans, smaller insurers and HMOs will go out of business, leaving the nation's medical future in the hands of the insurance giants. Managed competition will soon devolve into a system of quasi-monopolies. A few firms will set the parameters of "competition" among themselves.

Managed competition induced new schisms in the arcane world of Washington lobbyists. As the managed competition model emerged to dominate the health care reform agenda, the insurance industry's formidable lobby has split in two. Five of the largest insurers with heavy investments in managed care plans withdrew from the Health Insurance Association of America (HIAA) to form the Alliance for Managed Competition. The smaller insurance companies remaining in HIAA are now at bitter odds with their giant brethren who plan to monopolize the industry in the aftermath of any Clinton-style reforms. Finally, it must be noted that managed competition fails the test of experience. There is no functioning system of managed competition anywhere in the world. Why leap toward an unknown system when a functional system is working north of the border?

Besides single-payer and Clinton's employer mandate/managed competition plans, two other approaches developed powerful congressional backers. A coalition of right-wing Democrats and "moderate" Republicans came out in support of "pure" versions of managed competition—managed competition without employer mandates or the promise of universal coverage. It was a coalition which the Clinton administration appeared intent on propitiating. This group, led by Jim Cooper in the House of Representatives and Senators Chafee, Durenberger, Boren, and Breaux, would facilitate the formation of purchasing alliances, and offer modest subsidies for low income families, but would not require employers to provide coverage.

Finally, following the lead of William Kristol, former staffer to Vice President Dan Quayle, a large segment of the Republican party maintained that there was little need for reform. They proposed minimal insurance regulation to limit insurers' prerogatives to cancel policies and exclude the sick;

taxes on employer-funded health insurance to drive people into lower-cost plans; formation of voluntary alliances to facilitate group insurance purchasing; and caps on malpractice damage awards. They cite recent figures that suggest a slowing in health care inflation in 1994 as proof that there is no health care crisis. Unfortunately, the historical record suggests a "good behavior effect" on health care costs during times of national debate on health care reform. The last two times Congress toyed with the idea of national health insurance, in 1974 and 1979, private premium price increases almost slowed to the level of overall inflation. Once the crisis—for the insurance industry, that is—eased, the health care cost spiral accelerated again. Thus, current reports of sudden slowing in the level of health care cost increases should be viewed skeptically.

The few conservative Republicans who embrace universal coverage would get there by requiring everyone to purchase health insurance, much as car owners in many states must purchase auto insurance. Their plans assume that insurance, tax, and tort reforms would lower the cost of health insurance so dramatically that most people would be able to afford it. Many health professionals do practice defensive medicine out of fear of lawsuits, which in turn leads to unnecessary services. However, no serious estimate places the cost of malpractice damages at much more than 2 percent of the total cost of medicine, and the Congressional Budget Office (CBO) sees little chance that the Republican's projected savings can be realized. Hence few of the uninsured could afford coverage, and either tens of millions would remain uninsured, or massive government subsidies would be needed.

Similarly, the "moderate's" plan offered by Cooper and colleagues would, according to the CBO, leave twenty million or more uninsured, and cost far more than a single-payer reform. Moreover, the proposed government subsidies for the purchase of health insurance by low-income families, which this plan shares with many other "market-based" approaches, would create perverse tax incentives and might disrupt employment. Such plans would offer free coverage to the very poor (for example, those below the poverty line), and partial subsidies to the near poor, which would taper to zero for those with incomes at twice the poverty line. Families currently at the poverty line (and 18 percent of full-time workers earn poverty-level incomes) would gain little by working to double their incomes (perhaps at a second job), since up to 80 percent of their added pay would be consumed by taxes and loss of the health insurance subsidy. Moreover, employers currently providing coverage for their low-wage workers would have every incentive to drop the coverage, since the government subsidy would pick up the tab. Hence, the costs of subsidies would rise inexorably.

Giant corporations have not been idle as the Congress has debated these flawed alternatives. Spurred by Clinton's endorsement of market-based approaches, and the assurance that Congress would reject the single-payer alternative that would eliminate most profit making in health insurance, hospitals, and other health providers, the medical–financial complex has moved with astonishing speed to corporatize health care.

Merger mania has struck the hospital industry; hundreds of hospitals long controlled by their doctors and local businessmen are being absorbed by national conglomerates accountable only to Wall Street. Thousands of doctors each month are faced with ultimatums from HMOs: sell us your practice and become our employee, or be driven out of practice as your patients are forced into HMOs that require enrollees to go to one of the HMO's own doctors. HMOs are consolidating into a few giant plans controlled by the "big seven" insurers (whose number was recently whittled to six by the merger of Metropolitan Life and Travelers). Blue Cross plans are abandoning their not-for-profit status so they can sell stock to raise the massive funding needed to buy hospitals and doctors' practices in order to compete with HMOs. These developments presage our market-based medical future unless a single-payer plan is adopted: a few giant corporations managing health care for shareholders, not patients.

HEALTH CARE:
A COMMODITY OR A RIGHT?

According to the United Nations Universal Declaration of Human Rights, "Freedom of speech and belief and freedom from fear and want has been proclaimed as the highest aspiration of the common people . . . Everyone has the right to a standard of living adequate for the health and well-being of himself and of his family, including food, clothing, housing and medical care, and necessary social services, and the right to security in the event of unemployment, sickness, disability, widowhood, old age or other lack of livelihood in circumstances beyond his control." As one moves from the universal to the particular the essence of the debate over health care reform boils down to a very simple question. Is health care to be considered a commodity or a right? For decades policy makers in the United States have treated health care as a commodity to be bought and sold like cars or soap. It is time to establish a right to health care, just as the right to a public education was established two hundred years ago.

Proponents of managed competition argue that a fundamental problem with America's health delivery system is that Americans do not spend enough of their own money on health care. They argue that patients are too insulated from costs because their insurance pays most bills and government or an employer buys the insurance. Rep. Pete Peterson, a Florida Democrat, member of the Conservative Democratic Forum (CDF), and cosponsor of the CDF's managed competition proposal, articulated this view at a Washington gathering in February 1993, "[we have] never had a situation in this country where you walked into the doctor and asked how much it costs to have your tonsils out."[27] In order to hold down spending, patients should bear more of the costs of their care.

But Americans already pay higher out-of-pocket medical costs than Canadians or Europeans, yet they see the doctor less often, spend less time in the hospital, and have fewer procedures performed.[28] For the most part Americans receive *too little,* not too much care. The notion expressed by Peterson and other conservatives that insurance coverage overinsulates patients from the price of medical care is scapegoating the victim. The perverse logic underlying this argument blames the patient for a system that provides him or her inadequate care!

In a society as wealthy as the United States, no one should go without needed medical care. Yet, because our system treats health care as a commodity for purchase by those able to afford it rather than a universal right of citizenship, tens of millions of uninsured and underinsured Americans go without vital services. Each year, moreover, the number of Americans unable to afford care grows and with it the toll of financial ruin, premature death, and disability.

These are recent trends. During the 1960s, Congress and the Johnson Administration took tentative steps toward making health care a right by creating Medicaid and Medicare. Medicaid offered government insurance for about half of the poor, mainly women and children. Medicare established a partial health care safety net for elderly Americans. These two programs measurably improved the population's health. For about fifteen years, between the start of Medicare and Medicaid and the early 1980s, access to care, and morbidity and mortality rates, steadily improved. Between 1965 and 1980 the proportion of black women receiving early prenatal care increased 50 percent, while infant mortality rates among African-Americans declined by more than half. During the same period, the percentage of poor Americans who had not seen a physician in more than two years was halved. The proportion of health care costs paid out-of-pocket declined from 52 percent to 28 percent. Meanwhile, the infant mortality rate fell 4.6 percent per year, and overall death rates decreased 21 percent.

Unfortunately, inflation-adjusted per capita health spending doubled during those fifteen years in part because new and improved technology brought increased costs and because a much-needed expansion of medical care took place within the boundaries of an unduly expensive profit-based medical system. Beginning shortly before the election of Reagan to the presidency, American health care policy, both in government and private industry, came to focus solely on slowing cost growth. Private insurers raised deductibles and co-payments, expanded exclusions from coverage (for example, refusing to pay for "pre-existing" conditions) and intensified efforts to avoid insuring people with a high risk of illness. State governments threw people off Medicaid rolls and cut back coverage. While these policies have not contained costs, their toll has been high in terms of restrictions on care and inequalities in health. Decades of steady social progress and improvement in health standards have been halted, and, in many instances, reversed.

In the 1980's economic disparities in American society significantly increased. The Great Society social programs of the 1960s had reduced by half the proportion of Americans living below the poverty line. However, like many of the health gains, nearly all of these economic advances have been wiped out in the past fifteen years. At present 35.7 million Americans, 14.2 percent of the civilian population, live in poverty. The proportion of American children living in poverty had fallen from 26.5 percent in 1960 to 14.9 percent in 1970, but has risen again to 21.8 percent. In 1979, 12.1 percent of full time workers earned incomes below the poverty level. By 1990, the proportion had risen to 18 percent, affecting all races. In 1979, 18.5 percent of full-time black workers' incomes were below poverty levels; by 1990, the figure had risen to 25.3 percent. For white workers the figures rose from 11.4 percent (1979) to 17.1 percent (1990).[29]

Racial inequality is reflected in disparities of both income and health. As overall American poverty rates and mortality declined during the late 1960s and early 1970s, the gap between the black and the white infant mortality rate began to close, moving from a high of just under 2:1 in 1964 to less than 1.8 to 1 in 1974. With the retrenchment of the late 1970s and early 1980s, the gap began to increase again. By 1985, the ratio had increased back to 2:1, and reached record high levels in 1987 and 1989.[30]

A much greater proportion of the American population lives in poverty than in other wealthy industrialized nations; almost twice as high as in Canada and the U.K., and four times higher than in Sweden. The average income in the United States is as high as in these other countries; poverty in the United States results from extreme income inequalities. Since 1977 the wealthiest 1 percent of the American population has substantially increased its share of the national income, while the lower 60 percent of the population has actually experienced a decrease

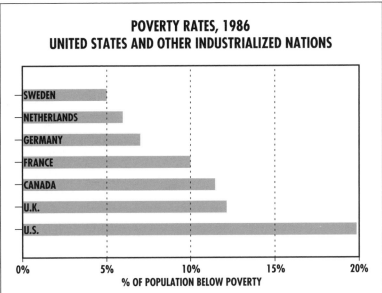

POVERTY RATES, 1986
UNITED STATES AND OTHER INDUSTRIALIZED NATIONS

% OF POPULATION BELOW POVERTY

Source: Data computed by John Coder, U.S. Census Bureau, based on Luxembourg Income Study Working Papers, cited in *Left Business Observer* 61, December 13, 1994.

A much higher proportion of the U.S. population lives in poverty than in other advanced industrialized societies. The percentage is nearly twice as high as in Canada and the United Kingdom, and four times higher than in Sweden. Since the average income in the United States is as high or higher than in these other nations, the high U.S. poverty rate is clearly the consequence of extreme income inequalities.

in real incomes. Pretax income increased about 80 percent, and aftertax income by 110 percent for the wealthiest 1 percent. At the same time, the poorest 20 percent of the population suffered a 15 percent loss in real income, and most middle-income Americans suffered modest declines as well. A single-payer system will not in itself alleviate the medical problems of the poor and racial minorities. Poverty is itself a primary cause of health problems. Nevertheless, aside from greatly improved access to health care, a National Health Program based on a single-payer system will have a positive impact on the income of the poorest classes. It will enable at least some parents to get off welfare because they no longer have to fear losing medicaid coverage for their children if they take a job which under present conditions may not offer health care coverage.

Thirty-nine million people, 14 percent of all Americans, were uninsured by 1992, more than at any time since the passage of Medicare and Medicaid. The number of uninsured increased 2 million between 1989 and 1991 alone. Overall, about 13 million more people are uninsured today than in 1980. The distribution of health insurance reflects wider social inequalities. Nearly one-third of the Hispanic population, 21 percent of African-Americans, and 11 percent of non-Hispanic whites were uninsured in 1992. While the poor and minority group members are most likely to be uninsured, substantial numbers of people from virtually all racial and ethnic groups lack coverage. Among those who are uninsured 5.3 million had family incomes above $50,000 per year, while an additional 7.2 million had family incomes between $25,000 and $50,000 annually.[31] Yet today, even having medical insurance does not guarantee security. Nearly all policies leave significant gaps in coverage, charge deductibles and co-payments, and cap lifetime benefits, assuring that anyone who is very sick for very long will be bankrupted.

The number of underinsured, like the number of uninsured, is rising. Many employers anxious to reduce health benefit costs have reduced the comprehensiveness of private insurance coverage and/or increased co-payments. In one notorious case the H&H Music Company of Houston, Texas, unilaterally slashed benefits for AIDS-related treatment when, in 1986, Jack McGann informed the company that he had AIDS. Under H & H's policy, he had been entitled to a lifetime maximum benefit of $1 million. However, when the policy came up for renewal, the company added a clause capping AIDS-related benefits at $5,000, a change that was upheld by the U.S. Supreme Court.

Any senior citizen who relies solely on Medicare is dangerously underinsured. Over the past decade Medicare co-payments for covered services have risen 50 percent faster than the elderly's incomes, and Medicare doesn't cover some services at all, including nursing homes and prescription drugs. These gaps force the elderly to spend an increasing proportion of their income on medical care. By 1988, the average senior was spending $2,394 a year for medical bills not covered by Medicare.[32] Seniors now spend 18.1 percent of their income on health care not covered by Medicare, a 50 percent increase in the proportion of income spent for medical care since 1977. Indeed, Medicare currently covers less than half of the medical expenses of the elderly, roughly the same proportion covered by private insurance before Medicare was created.

The entire Clinton approach to cost control created a serious political dilemma when it came to Medicare. Medicare relies primarily on traditional "fee-for-service" reimbursement, and recipients are therefore accustomed to choosing their own physician without financial penalties. The largest out-of-pocket expense for the elderly is the cost of pharmaceuticals, which are not currently covered by Medicare. Despite the substantial deductibles, by themselves the proposed drugs benefits in the Clinton plan would represent a substantial improvement in coverage for the elderly. That is, if the rest of Medicare were to remain unchanged. However, should the elderly be shifted *en masse* to a proposed Clinton style alliance structure, those who opt for fee-for-service plans will find themselves facing out-of-pocket costs at least as high as they currently face under Medicare. Thus, what the Clintons would give in drug benefits, they would take away in the form of high deductibles or constrained choice under managed care. The single-payer plan, on the other hand, would provide an unequivocal improvement in benefits for the elderly.

A Canadian-style single-payer system would best achieve the goal of universal health care. It would be based on the premise that health care is a right of citizenship, not a commodity. We do not buy national defense or primary education based on what the market will provide; government acquires these goods on behalf of the public. Thus, both are perceived to be "public goods" funded through public means. As with basic education and national security, the essential right to quality health care must be assured.

Under a single-payer plan, everyone would get a national health insurance card at birth entitling them to walk into any hospital or doctor's office in the country and get the care needed, without any out-of-pocket payment. When people pay their tax bill, they will have paid their health insurance premium. It is by far the simplest, most cost-efficient, and rational of all the approaches under debate. The average tax payment will be lower than the current cost of private insurance premiums.

The idea of a "health security card," advanced in the program of Physicians for a National Health Plan, was such a compelling image that Clinton appropriated the idea, and now brandishes his own card. But the Clinton approach and the single-payer approach are quite different. For employed people, the Clinton card would require the holder to pay 20 percent of the insurance premium (100 percent if self-employed). Individuals would face strong pressures to join an HMO, since outside of HMOs, insurers could charge up to $3,000 per family per year ($1,500 for individuals) in out-of-pocket expenses for covered services and an additional 20 percent co-payment for prescription drugs.[33] The guaranteed benefits package would cover little long-term care, and severely restrict mental health, dental, and eye care. The Clinton Administration's proposed coverage was so skimpy that the administration decided not to offer it to senior citizens, at least initially, since it would represent a downgrading of Medicare. In press reports, administration officials frankly admitted that the decision to preserve Medicare arose because of fear of a political "backlash" if senior citizens were folded into the new system.

THE RATIONAL OPTION

Defining a new right to health care poses difficult questions for a society facing many crises. In the face of other pressing social problems, can we afford to create a massive new federal program that offers everyone in America coverage? Not only *can* the United States financially afford to enact a National Health Program, we can no longer rationally afford not to establish such a system. Although public-opinion polls consistently show that a majority of Americans favor a shift to a single-payer plan, the opposition to such reform quips that "government efficiency" is an oxymoron.

Not only are the coverage and benefits offered under Physicians for a National Health Program's single-payer proposal far more generous, they are also more cost-efficient than any other reform proposal under debate. Even assuming the Clinton plan had managed to cobble together minimal coverage for everyone by maintaining a hybrid public/private system and clinging to the belief that competition will control costs, the administration's proposal would have foregone enormous savings. Of the proposals offered in the last Congress, including a managed competition bill, the CBO concluded that single payer offered the best prospects by far for cost control. The CBO projected an initial increase in national health expenditures under single payer, as people took advantage of new access to health care. However, even while adopting a conservative estimate of the administrative savings to be reaped from switching to single payer, CBO projected at least $114 billion in savings, or 5.5 percent of projected national health expenditures of slightly more than $2 trillion by the year 2003.[34] While not as optimistic as the GAO study noted earlier, CBO affirmed that "the administrative savings from switching to a single-payer system would offset some of the cost of the additional services demanded by consumers."[35]

Managed competition theorists believe that the sum of millions of individual choices within a market economy will add up to social efficiency. In medical care, however, market theory fails. Market theory's prediction, for instance, that an increase in the number of doctors or medical facilities would lower prices has proven false. As noted earlier, medical enterprises routinely duplicate facilities and equipment within a single region in order to attract patients to their facilities. The end result of this oversupply is higher, not lower, costs. The individual profit-maximizing behavior of medical enterprises thus conflicts with society's interest in efficiency. Moreover, when patients act as cost-conscious consumers of health care, they frequently end up costing society more in the long run. If short-term financial considerations stop an individual from using preventive and primary medical care (for example, treatment of high blood pressure), the problem may progress to a later stage (for instance, a stroke) when therapy is much more expensive, and less effective.

The insurance industry and its paid policy "experts" have tried to frighten Americans away from a single-payer system by claiming that the Canadian health care system promotes bureaucracy, long waiting lines for services, and draconian rationing. These myths play into traditional American prejudices against government. Yet, the Canadian system is remarkably lean, efficient, and fair, while the private American system drastically rations services, essentially according to income, and wastes tens of billions of dollars on unnecessary bureaucracy and overhead.

The United States expends extraordinary amounts of

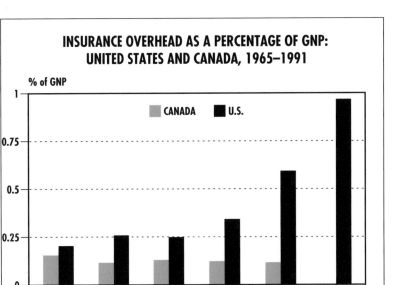

INSURANCE OVERHEAD AS A PERCENTAGE OF GNP: UNITED STATES AND CANADA, 1965–1991

Source: International OECD Database (Paris: Organization for Economic Cooperation and Development, 1993); S. W. Letsch, "National Health Care Spending in 1991," *Health Affairs*, 12 (1993), 94–110.

Health insurance overhead alone now accounts for 1 percent of Gross National Product in the United States, as compared to about 0.1 percent of GNP in Canada. United States private insurers keep, on average, more than 12 percent of total premium dollars for their overhead and profits. That is, for every dollar of premium paid, more than 12 cents stays with the insurance company and less than 88 cents goes towards clinical care. Total insurance overhead in the United States approached fifty billion dollars in 1992. In contrast to the United States, Canada's provincial insurance plans run for an overhead of less than 1 percent, instead of 12 percent, of total costs.

money and effort administering its health care system, and the bureaucratic waste is multiplying. Between 1970 and 1991 the number of health care administrators in the United States increased by 697 percent. In the same period the total number of health care personnel increased by only 129 percent.[36] The costs of health insurance overhead, hospital and nursing home administration, and doctors' office overhead amounted to $159.1 billion in 1991, 21 percent of all health care spending.

Contrary to conventional wisdom, private insurers spend

far more on bureaucracy than do government insurance programs. Americans paid the fifteen hundred private insurance companies $241.5 billion for premiums during 1991. Those companies paid out $209.2 billion in benefits. The remaining $32.3 billion, more than 13 percent of every premium dollar, went for overhead—claims processing, marketing, building and furnishing insurance company offices, executives' salaries, and, of course, perks and profits.[37] In contrast, Medicare spent about 2 percent on administration. Insurance overhead in Canada's public insurance system takes less than one cent of each premium dollar. The economic rationality of the Canadian system is irrefutable.

In the United States fifteen hundred different insurance companies, along with Medicaid, Medicare, and employer-provided plans, pay hospitals, doctors, and laboratories. This multi-payer structure has spawned a complex system of accounting because each "payer" (that is, insurance company or government agency) has its own rules and documentation requirements, and tries to shift costs onto other payers. The result is a stifling administrative burden for American medical professionals and hospitals, and the creation of an army of accountants and administrators to sift through billing paperwork. Again the contrast between the United States and Canada is sharp. A typical Canadian hospital's billing department employs about three people, mainly to send bills to Americans who wander across the border. In contrast, a typical American hospital employs fifty people to process bills. Detailed Medicare records for 6,400 hospitals nationwide, obtained through the Freedom of Information Act, show that in 1990, 24.8 percent of all hospital spending in the United States went to administration.[38]

The Canadian system pays hospitals on a lump sum basis, as we pay fire departments in the United States, eliminating per-patient billing, and hence the need to attribute costs for each aspirin tablet to individual patients and insurers. As a result Canadian hospitals spend little on billing and internal cost tracking, and between 9 and 11 percent of their total budgets on administration, less than half of current U.S. spending.[39] Winnowing the number of insurers to a handful, as promised under managed competition, would save little on hospital billing, and nothing on hospitals' internal cost tracking.

There are no precise figures for the time and expense devoted to administration in physicians' offices. In 1991, American physicians incurred professional expenses of $66 billion, 45 percent of their gross income. Nearly half of all people employed in doctor's offices (47 percent) are clerical and secretarial staff. Much of their time goes to tasks that do not exist in Canada, patient and third-party billing. Administrative costs are rising even more rapidly than overall health care costs. In the most recent year for which we have figures, overall health care spending went up 10.3 percent and medical bureaucracy costs increased 16.4 percent.[40]

For-profit (proprietary) insurance companies and hospitals also accumulate billions of dollars in annual profits. Profits in this instance represent health spending above the actual cost of care. Most economic theorists assume that profits are the result of efficiency, and that consumers in a profit-motivated system benefit from well-made goods and excellent service. However, no evidence suggests that proprietary hospitals provide better care than nonprofit hospitals. In fact, the scant available evidence points to the opposite conclusion.

A single-payer system would obviate many administrative tasks including eligibility testing, as when people move on and off Medicaid or thousands of different private insurance programs. In a bizarre tug of war, Congress has repeatedly tried to expand the number of people eligible for Medicaid without offering sufficient federal funding. States, in turn, have tried to find ways around providing coverage, leading to a complex enrollment and eligibility process. The need for constant eligibility testing drives Medicaid administrative costs up over 3.5 percent. Medicare recipients, on the other hand, once enrolled are in forever, and Medicare overhead last year was only 1.9 percent. A single-payer system would enroll everyone at birth, eliminating one of the major administrative tasks (and costs) of Medicaid and private insurance.

In health care, as in many things, simplicity is a virtue. The GAO estimated the difference in bureaucratic costs between the complex U.S. system and Canada's simple one at 9 percent of health spending, equivalent to $99 billion in 1994.[41] Based on the more recent Medicare data on hospital administrative spending, we estimate the bureaucratic savings from switching to a single-payer system to be at least $117.7 billion annually, slightly more than half of current spending on health care bureaucracy.

The numbers prove the inefficiency of private insurance. The record of Medicare shows that the federal government already does the job far more efficiently than the private sector. The astonishing gap in efficiency between private insurers and public programs contradicts the conventional wisdom in Washington. How can private insurance be so inefficient and a government program so efficient?

The answer can only be found in understanding what an insurance company is and how it compares with other business enterprises. Private insurance companies are generally for-profit corporations or partnerships, as are most of the companies that "self insure" their employees. In either case, executives' top priority must be producing profits for their shareholders. (Though some large insurance companies are mutuals, that is, nominally owned by policyholders, they behave as if they were for-profit corporations.) The managers of the corporation are legally bound to place the profit-seeking interests of shareholders above those of employees or patients. An insurance or business executive who did otherwise would face a shareholder's lawsuit.

Thus access to health care for patients must be secondary. When the need to produce profits collides with the patients' need for health care, it is care that must give way. The American health care system is unfair and bureaucratic not because of selfishness or moral failure of insurance executives, but because of the very nature of the private health insurance business. Managed-care plans owned by insurance companies must pressure providers to give less care. Thus organizing all health care around the profit motive creates ethical conflicts between patients and providers that will further compromise the already beleaguered doctor-patient relationship. Patients unable to fend for themselves because of (young or old) age or infirmity are most at risk.

The notion of ousting the insurance industry from its controlling perch above the nation's health care carries strong popular appeal, a fact not lost on the Clintons. Indeed, Hillary Rodham Clinton has rhetorically exploited the unpopularity of the insurance industry. Yet her attacks on "greedy insurance companies" implied that some insurance companies are not motivated solely by pecuniary gain; that reforms could root out the unethical firms and encourage a few high-minded insurance companies to carry on. It is thus that Hillary Clinton could, with a straight face, promise a "populist crusade" against medical "profiteers" on behalf of a managed competition proposal designed to deepen the insurance giants' control over American medicine.

Why would competition not enhance quality or cut costs in health care? First, while prevention improves health and may cut costs ten years down the line, insurers operate on a much shorter time-frame. Since competition encourages patients to switch plans frequently (if patients do not switch to the lower-cost plans then managed competition theory makes no sense at all), the savings from prevention would likely accrue to a competitor's plan. Moreover, carving up health care among fierce competitors undermines the most effective prevention and quality improvement strategies, which require a community-wide purview. For instance, cutting fat intake to decrease heart disease requires intervening in school lunch programs, prevailing on stores to offer low-fat products, working with restaurants to increase the availability of low-fat meals, and so forth. Plans that invest in such programs would actually be at a competitive disadvantage since they would incur costs, but benefits would accrue to their competitors. Similarly, a plan that pioneered a new surgical technique that would cut costs and improve care would lose by sharing its innovation with competitors. Quality improvements would become trade secrets hidden from competitors, rather than scientific discoveries spread with missionary zeal.

Insurers/HMOs also find more profit in marketing and gaming the system than in real cost cutting or quality improvement. Ten percent of the population consumes 72 percent of health care. Hence, the surest way to undercut competitors is to attract the healthy and avoid enrolling the sick, or drive them away with unsatisfactory care. The subtle and varied methods of risk selection defy effective regulation: place sign-up offices on upper floors of buildings with malfunctioning elevators; refuse contracts to providers in neighborhoods with high rates of HIV (an example of medical redlining); structure salary scales to assure a high turnover among physicians—the longer they are in practice, the more sick patients they accumulate; provide luxurious services (even exercise-club membership) for the well, and shabby inconvenience for those with expensive chronic illnesses.

Such cream skimming is costly as well as unfair. Even the most efficient plan that fails to risk-select could not compete against less efficient but risk-selecting rivals. Moreover, insurers with low-risk enrollees do not pass on the full savings to enrollees. Instead they "shadow price," charge premiums below the competition but well above costs. As a result society pays twice: once for the high-risk people concentrated in high-cost plans, and again for the excess profits in plans that succeed in risk-selection.

Clinton's plan would have augmented these traditional insurance scams with such new games as "capitation creep." His Health Alliances would pay higher premiums to the plans for sick patients. Clever insurance executives could inflate their enrollees' risk profile by running batteries of unproven screening tests on all plan members, dubiously labeling millions with premium-inflating diagnoses such as "borderline diabetes" or "early Alzheimer's."

Offering billions as reward to unscrupulous managed care entrepreneurs, Clinton would temper their zeal with a regulatory apparatus sure to be out matched by the industry itself. Insurance regulators have failed to prevent even gross financial fraud (for instance, in New York's Empire Blue Cross) and flagrant patient abuse (for example, by the largest HMOs participating in Medicare's HMO Demonstration Project, which enticed seniors with images of luxurious care, and then refused to provide even rudimentary care while the owners absconded with the Medicare dollars).[42] The Byzantine complexity of Clinton's plan would have opened more loopholes than its arcane regulatory structure could possibly plug.

Increasing numbers of individuals already find themselves marooned in an insurance "no man's land." People who lose or change jobs and have a "pre-existing condition" are often denied private medical insurance. The cruel paradox of private health insurance is that it is "bad business" to insure those who are ill and in the greatest need of medical care. And when a privately insured person develops a chronic illness, insurance companies often make care inconvenient or even unobtainable through denials of reasonable claims or refusals to authorize essential procedures. Thus the chronically ill are often hounded out of private insurance plans and into government programs such as Medicare or Medicaid.

Under the Clinton plan, insurers would have been required to offer coverage to anyone who applies, cover pre-existing conditions, and charge each customer the same "community rate." (Community rating means calculating the expected health costs for a population and charging everyone the same amount.) Behind "community rating" is a belief that insurance should work to socialize risk, that is, spread the unpredictable costs of illness over the entire population—both ill and healthy.

In the past two decades cheap computer power has made a plethora of health data available to insurers. More and more, insurance companies can predict the future health needs of individuals based on past health history, lifestyle, and demography. With such information at hand, they can identify poor risks, and try to avoid them. Private insurers have thus shifted from socializing risk to charging individuals and groups in advance for expected services, thereby standing the traditional concept of "insurance" on its head.[43] In Canada, the single-payer system pools risks across the entire province and offers a true community rate, without the need for a cat and mouse game between government regulators and profit-driven insurance companies.

Insurers' scams to push the sick into competitors' plans and jack up their share of premium dollars is a major form of "cost shifting," which the Clintons have decried.[44] But just as the Clintons' rhetoric on greedy insurance firms falsely implies the existence of ungreedy insurers, so the rhetoric on cost shifting implies that cost shifting is somehow an aberration in the health insurance market. In fact, socially undesirable "cost shifting" is endemic to a competitive insurance market; by definition, insurance companies work to shift costs to other competitors, individuals, or government in order to increase profits.

Companies that offer health insurance to their employees complain that competitors who do not are "shifting costs" unfairly. Yet by forcing ever-higher co-payments and deductibles on their employees, employers engage in a form of cost shifting as well. Higher co-payments and deductibles disproportionately penalize the sick. In the name of "personal responsibility," the White House proposal explicitly endorsed this "sick-tax." When the systemic cost control fails under the Clinton plan or any other market-based "reform," then employers will predictably demand the right to shift more costs onto their employees. Insurance should perform socially desirable cost shifting by spreading the costs of illness over a broad pool of people, healthy as well as sick. A single-payer system performs this critical social function explicitly, fairly, without apology, and with a minimum of waste.

Rationing

Opponents of single-payer systems raise the bugaboo of "rationing" to scare Americans. Waiting lists for services in Canada receive a tremendous amount of publicity in the United States but, in fact, Canadians only occasionally wait for a handful of expensive high-tech procedures. In a study done in the Province of Ontario, the GAO of the U.S. Congress found significant queues for emergency cases only in lithotripsy (sound-wave treatment of kidney stones).[45] The GAO also concluded that "primary care is easily accessible to Ontario residents. Patients visit their family physician or other general practitioner with no evident queues or lengthy waiting times for appointments." Moreover, the GAO has concluded that the substantial surplus of high-tech equipment and services in the United States would obviate any need for queuing in the short run under an American single-payer system.[46]

It is essential, however, to compare the heavily publicized Canadian record on queues and waiting lists with the record of American medicine. As noted above, the National Medical Expenditure Survey found that in 1987, a million Americans needed emergency attention and never got it. Long queues in emergency departments (EDs) are common in both public and private hospitals in the United States. In a nationwide survey of hospital EDs in August 1988, the average ED reported transferring patients to other facilities on 7 percent of all days, and turning away ambulances on 12 percent of all days. Long waits for admission and ED crowding were as common at private as at public hospitals.[47]

The myth of Canadian shortages pervades the American health care debate. Paul Tsongas, former senator from Massachusetts and then presidential candidate, dismissed the idea of a single-payer system by pointing to his own cancer treatment. Tsongas told reporters that Canadian-style systems stifle research, and that if the United States had such a system he might have died for lack of a bone-marrow transplant to treat his lymphoma. In fact, one of the critical research break-throughs that led to bone-marrow transplants was made in Toronto during the early 1960s.[48] As for availability, Canadians receive bone-marrow transplants more often than Americans do. Between 1988 and 1990, Canadians received bone-marrow transplants at the rate 9.1 per million people, while in the United States the rate was 7.5 per million.[49]

The American system rations by income and insurance status. About one-third of all Americans are either uninsured or underinsured. Many of them face grave difficulties in getting needed care, and they are sicker and die younger because of this poor access to care. Lack of insurance is a strong predictor of failure to get needed medical care. The uninsured, regardless of income, spend fewer days in the hospital and see doctors less frequently than comparable insured persons, according to data from the National Health Interview Survey.

An increasing proportion of Americans report avoiding care because of costs, 27 percent in 1981 versus 36 percent in 1987.[50] The proportion of the population that avoids medical care because of costs is nearly three times greater than the proportion of those who are uninsured, and financial barriers to access affect insured Americans. According to a 1986 Robert Wood Johnson Foundation Survey, 12 percent of all insured adults under the age of sixty-five who had a serious or chronic illness experienced a major financial problem due to illness within the last year. A further 19 percent had failed to see a doctor, and 15 percent had failed to secure necessary medication, physical therapy, or other ancillary services because of the expense.[51]

Delaying essential care causes suffering and can be fatal. In Massachusetts, researchers asked hospitalized patients if their hospitalization had been delayed. The uninsured poor were twice as likely as those with private insurance to report a delay of hospital care, while those with HMO coverage reported slightly more delays than those with traditional private insurance. Among those delaying care, hospital stays were longer and death rates higher than for patients without delays, even after adjustment for age and diagnosis.[52]

The United States rations care within the context of staggering surpluses of hospital beds, medical equipment, and physician specialists. All of the services for which the GAO found queues in Canada—MRI, lithotripsy, cardiovascular surgery, orthopedic surgery—are available in the United States in irrational excess while at the same time people in need of primary services go unattended. A Rand Corporation study found that little more than half of heart bypass surgery in the United States was of clear medical benefit. Rand also found that only a third of surgeries to bypass blocked blood vessels in the neck (carotid endarterectomy) were clearly beneficial.[53] Similarly, the vast duplication of mammography facilities has driven up the cost per test, making mammography less rather than more available.

INSURANCE GATEKEEPERS ARE RATIONING AGENTS

Despite this oversupply of facilities, the American health care system raises nonfinancial as well as financial barriers to care. The Clinton Administration's proposal relied heavily on managed care. HMOs and other managed care networks rely on "gatekeepers"—primary care physicians, physicians' assistants, nurse practitioners, insurance company bureaucrats—to control patients' access to diagnostic and specialty services. The gatekeepers and the rules they apply are rationing. Patients in managed care arrangements often must wait to see approved specialists or to get appointments at approved diagnostic and treatment centers. During the course of therapy, they must return often to the gatekeeper to get approval for more therapy, creating further delay. A Harris poll of patients in the United States and Canada revealed a remarkable statistic: Americans were twice as likely to report ostensibly nonfinancial barriers to care as were Canadians.[54]

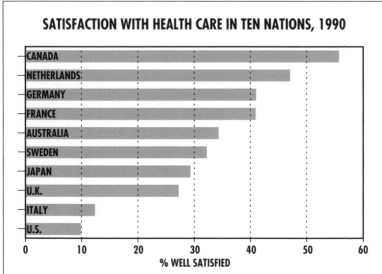

SATISFACTION WITH HEALTH CARE IN TEN NATIONS, 1990

CANADA

NETHERLANDS

GERMANY

FRANCE

AUSTRALIA

SWEDEN

JAPAN

U.K.

ITALY

U.S.

0   10   20   30   40   50   60

% WELL SATISFIED

Source: R.J. Blendon et al. "Satisfaction With Health Systems in Ten Nations," *Health Affairs* 9 (1990), 185–92.

The Harris polling organization surveyed random samples of the population in each of ten advanced industrial nations. Canadians were the most satisfied with their care while Americans trailed all the other nations.

Managed care, in theory, assigns each patient a chaperone through the system, to insure that all necessary services are received in the most cost-effective manner. Again the theory and reality often differ. While some HMOs provide good care, many use the gatekeeper system to bully doctors and patients out of needed care. Particularly vulnerable are patients lacking knowledge or resources needed to work the system (for example, being able to hold thirty minutes on a telephone during the workday because the HMO has purposefully kept appointment desk staffing low). A major Rand Corporation study found that poor people who get sick have worse outcomes in HMOs than in fee-for-service care.[55]

The Clinton Administration paints a rosy image of universal coverage based on clones of today's best HMOs. But managed competition is unlikely to reproduce top-quality con-sumer-responsive plans like the Group Health Cooperative of Puget Sound, or even Kaiser, for everyone. Bay State HMO in Massachusetts offers a more realistic glimpse into the future. The plan suddenly fired hundreds of psychiatrists in 1993. Their patients were instructed to call the HMO's 800 number and describe their psychiatric difficulties; a new mental health provider would be assigned. Under Massachusetts Medicaid's managed competition-style selective contracting, mental health services are covered. But in the city of Springfield, contracts were denied to all Spanish-speaking providers, and even to those with translators. Similarly in Cambridge, an alcoholic in withdrawal has to travel at least forty minutes for Medicaid-financed care, passing a dozen hospitals en route. Technically, the service is covered, but nonfinancial obstacles mean that few can readily access it.

Managed care is overloaded with cost watchdogs looking over doctors' shoulders. In New Jersey, Prudential's managed care plan, PruCare, provides coverage to 110,000 people. According to the *New York Times,* PruCare employs five physi-cian reviewers, (four of them part time), eighteen nurse review-ers, eight provider recruiters, fifteen sales representatives, twenty-seven service representatives, and one hundred clerks, excluding the staff at Prudential headquarters.[56]

Staff and group model HMOs control costs by skimping on doctors. On average, HMOs employ one doctor for each 800 patients enrolled. For the population as a whole, the patient/doctor ratio is approximately 400 to 1. Hence, the Clin-ton Administration's proposed HMO expansion would absorb many patients but few physicians. The result would be a glut of doctors, primarily specialists, in private practice serving a shrinking pool of patients. Initially, doctors might increase fees to meet their overhead and maintain their incomes, but increas-ing fees would accelerate movement of patients into HMOs. If half of Americans enrolled in health maintenance organizations with one doctor per 800 patients (and competition would push

HMOs to keep physician staffing to a minimum, Kaiser has recently increased to 2,000 the number of patients assigned to each primary care doctor), each remaining private physician would serve an average of only 267 patients, too few to cover even office overhead.

At a certain point, private practice would implode, leaving tens of thousands of doctors scrambling for work. At the limit, if all Americans enrolled in HMOs, roughly 275,000 doctors, most of them specialists, would be stranded in a private practice sector devoid of patients. Competition for HMO jobs would be fierce, the disruption of care massive. How much more rational to use our physician "surplus" to lengthen the average patient visit from the current seven minutes to fifteen.

The high co-payments and deductibles in the Clinton fee-for-service option would force most patients into managed care, and shrink the fee-for-service sector, ultimately forcing patients and doctors to enter the most restrictive form of care. No amount of "spin" control or repetition of the word "choice" can alter this conclusion. The Clinton proposals will leave doctors and patients with the sham choice between one or another corporate-owned HMO.

Clearly, American specialist physicians will have to make some financial sacrifices as part of any health care reform. In 1941, American doctors earned 3.5 times the income of the average worker. By 1990, the ratio had climbed to 6, with doctors' incomes averaging $164,300 and many earning much more.[57] Physician fees have held a constant percentage of national health expenditures over the past three decades, but that still means physician income has increased at twice the rate of general inflation. Primary care physicians in the United States and Canada make roughly the same incomes, while many categories of U.S. specialists have far higher incomes than their Canadian counterparts. Since the physician mix in the United States is weighted so heavily to specialty care, the overall gap between physician expenditures in the two countries is substantial.

The United States needs to shift service delivery from specialty to primary care, and to control the growth of physician income. But must we force patients into the arms of CIGNA, Aetna, and substandard HMOs, and touch off a desperate scramble among physicians for jobs? A survey by Metropolitan Life found that an overwhelming majority of physicians would readily accept a ten percent reduction in income in exchange for less paperwork or less utilization review. The Clinton proposal's central cost control strategy promised a vast increase in utilization review and other burdensome managed care procedures. This route cannot deliver any significant reduction in paperwork, and will almost certainly increase bureaucratic costs and waste.

The Clintons' "spin doctors" trumpeted a new, pluralistic health care system, filled with patient "choice" and contented doctors freed from micro-management. Yet, a closer look revealed a system dominated by the utilization reviewers implementing the directives of an ever more powerful insurance industry cartel. The Clinton proposals would simply have given federal sanction to the corporate transformation of American medicine already proceeding apace.

Under the single-payer alternative, patients would have complete freedom to choose their doctors. Similarly, doctors would be free to choose their practice style. The financial savings would arise from the enormous administrative simplification achieved by evicting the insurance industry from the medical system. The delivery of medical services under the single-payer option would be shifted toward primary and preventive care, with minimal disruption of care. Although some specialists would see a reduction in income under either approach, the Canadian model would do it more gradually and predictably, while ensuring much greater clinical freedom for patients.

If the American system of rationing was genuinely a consequence of shortages of resources it might be acceptable as a tragic necessity. However, within the context of empty hospital beds, oversupply and underutilization of existing technology, and a plethora of pointless surgery, such rationing is not only morally repugnant, it is unnecessary.

The American Medical Association (AMA), Dan Quayle, and others have argued that malpractice damage awards drive the health care cost spiral. In fact, they do not. Although malpractice premiums have skyrocketed, they constitute "considerably less than 1 percent of total medical spending."[58] Nevertheless, there is need for reform in the area of malpractice. Many physicians order procedures of dubious value as a method of defending themselves in advance from malpractice accusations. The AMA suggests that defensive medicine costs between $15 and $30 billion a year. Those figures are based on methodologically poor studies. What is known is that direct costs of malpractice premiums are small. According to a 1992 AMA survey, doctors' malpractice premiums on average consumed only 3.5 percent of their practice receipts.[59]

The overheated rhetoric on the costs of defensive medicine and frivolous lawsuits distracts attention from a genuine malpractice crisis. A comprehensive Harvard study of malpractice in the state of New York suggests that medical negligence harms more than 300,000 patients annually and kills 80,000. Yet, only 30,000 suits are brought each year, most of which are frivolous. The wrong doctors get sued for the wrong cases. While 8 percent of doctors are sued each year, relatively few cases get to trial, and fewer than three hundred verdicts end up favoring the patients. Patients and doctors lose in this system.[60]

Attorneys and insurance companies are the main beneficiaries. Between 66 and 80 percent of malpractice premiums are consumed by insurance overhead and legal costs. A national health program should include systematic malpractice reform and, more important, initiatives to prevent medical negligence. Tort reform, such as a cap on damages or the imposition of ruinous attorneys' fees for unsuccessful plaintiffs, leaves the current system intact while punishing both real victims and frivolous plaintiffs. There is no evidence that health care costs have risen any less steeply in the several states that have enacted tort reform. A national no-fault system for medical errors or injuries, modeled on the Swedish malpractice system or New Zealand's accident compensation system, would compensate patients more fairly and reduce legal fees. No-fault malpractice systems compensate anyone who is injured during medical care, without the patient having to prove negligence.

THE DREADED "T" WORD

A single-payer system holds costs down in three ways. First, it eliminates tens of billions of dollars worth of unnecessary bureaucracy. Second, it provides the simplest method of setting national spending limits. (The Clinton proposals would have created an accounting nightmare, trying to impose a global budget on a system with dozens or hundreds of insurers and 250 million Americans each paying part of the bill. The bureaucratic task of keeping track would be monumental.) Finally, a single-payer system allows health planning to stop costly duplication of high technology services. Without a single source of payment, the implementation of serious cost control measures will remain elusive. However, with a single-payer system the nation's health care resources can be allocated efficiently and fairly, as has been done in both Europe and Canada.

Creating a single-payer national health program would eliminate health insurance premiums but require new taxes. The NHP would continue to spend the amounts now devoted to Medicare and Medicaid, and would have to receive new revenues to cover the uninsured and privately insured. There are many ways to do this; a graduated income tax or some other form of progressive taxation is the fairest.

During a transition period, continued funding that mimics existing spending patterns would minimize economic disruption. Congress would set funding at the same percent of GNP spent on health care the year before the NHP goes into effect. A tax earmarked for the NHP would be levied on all employers, with the rate set so that total collections equaled the previous year's total for employer's expenditures for health benefits, adjusted for inflation. Additional taxes equal to or less than the amount now spent by individuals for insurance premiums and out-of-pocket costs would be levied.

There will be an increase in overall health care costs for the first few years of the NHP as the elderly obtain long-term care and those without coverage are able to gain access to the medical system. However, in ensuing years the NHP would hold down cost increases to the level of GNP growth. Within a short period of time, the NHP would cost Americans considerably less than would either the status quo or the managed competition proposals. With health care costs projected at one trillion dollars in 1994, each American paid an estimated $4,000 in premiums, co-payments, deductibles, federal taxes for Medicaid and Medicare, property taxes to fund health care for municipal workers and so on. By the year 2000, without serious reform, we will spend 18 percent of GNP on health care, about $5,000 per person in 1994 dollars. Americans are certainly intelligent enough to know which is better: paying $5,000 to five or six different institutions for health care coverage with enormous gaps, or $4,000 in earmarked taxes for guaranteed comprehensive care. It is, as Thomas Paine once noted, common sense.

The United States came close to passing national health insurance during the 1970s. Opponents argued that the United States could not afford it. Canada, by contrast, completed implementation of its national health program in 1971. Until that time, United States and Canadian health spending, as a percent of GNP, were almost identical, and had been increasing at the same rate for decades. Since 1971 the United States has run its tab up to 14 percent of GNP. In comparison Canada's costs have leveled off at 9.5 percent of GNP. The United States cannot afford to adopt anything but a single-payer system.

Americans like to see themselves as hard-headed pragmatists, making decisions based on merits. Yet, faced with a need to reform a second-rate health care system, the Clintons offered

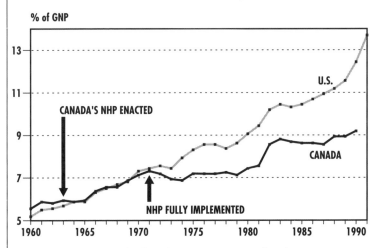

HEALTH COSTS AS A PERCENTAGE OF GNP: UNITED STATES AND CANADA, 1960–1991

% of GNP

CANADA'S NHP ENACTED

U.S.

CANADA

NHP FULLY IMPLEMENTED

Source: National Health Expenditures, 1975–1993 (Ottawa: Health Canada, 1994)
and *U.S. Industrial Outlook* (Washington: Department of Commerce, 1993)

The main argument used against national health insurance in the early 1970s was that we could not afford it. We now have clear evidence that a national health program is the most effective means of cost containment. American and Canadian health care costs, as a percentage of GNP, were almost identical until the full implementation of the Canadian national health program in 1971. Since that time, Canadian costs have leveled off at about 9 percent of GNP, while United States costs have increased to 14 percent of GNP, and continue to rise. Canada dramatically outperforms the United States on every front. In 1991 it provided universal coverage to all its citizens at five percent less of its GNP than the United States spent on a system which left nearly forty million of its citizens without insurance. Moreover, a clear majority of Canadians indicated satisfaction with their system while 90 percent of the population in the United States expressed dissatisfaction with the American system of health care.

A single-payer system facilitates cost containment in three ways. First, it can achieve substantial administrative savings that are not attainable under a multiple-payer system. Second, the single-payer system is easily able to set and enforce overall budgetary limits. Effectively limiting the overall health budget is extremely difficult under our multiple-payer system with 1,200 different private insurers, and more than 200 million Americans paying health bills. Finally, a single-payer system facilitates health planning to eliminate duplication of facilities and expensive technology that often wastes money and sometimes worsens quality. For instance, U.S. hospitals average only 65 percent occupancy; we have 10,000 mammography machines when only 5,000 would be needed to perform every test recommended for every woman in the nation; and so many hospitals perform open heart surgery that many do too few procedures to maintain their competence.

Americans a second-rate reform. Americans ought to be wise enough to throw prejudices aside and choose a system that has proven it can affordably provide universal coverage. The Clinton managed competition proposals represented an untried hypothetical idea riddled with deep flaws. Pragmatists drawn toward common sense solutions should favor a system that establishes health care as a right while at the same time jealously guarding the national purse. We must also be prepared to oppose the insurance industry and other powerful vested interests in this country that would deny us this choice.

Making all care free at the time of service would improve America's health. In the 1970s the Rand Corporation conducted a health insurance experiment, HIE for short, to determine the effects of various types of health insurance on health and cost. The HIE randomly assigned 2,005 families to different health insurance plans and measured the health and cost outcomes over three to five years. Several plans required co-payments, and one had completely free care, (unlimited access to medical care without deductibles or co-payments).[61] In other words, the free-care group had access similar to that within a Canadian-style system.

Families assigned free care, as one might expect, had more ambulatory visits, more hospital admissions, and higher medical expenses than families with co-payment plans. The study excluded populations with the highest risk of dying: newborns, the elderly and the chronically ill. As a result, very few people in the study died, and although the difference was statistically insignificant, both adults and children who were given free care had slightly lower death rates.

Rand researchers calculated the future risk of dying for each person in the study, based on blood pressure, smoking habits, weight, and serum cholesterol. When researchers focused on the 25 percent of the people in the study with the highest risk factors at the start of the experiment, they found that free access to medical care reduced the risk of dying by a statistically significant 10 percent.

The Rand study adopted a conservative assumption, that free care would have no greater health benefit for the highest-risk people in society (who were excluded altogether from the HIE), than for the low-risk people studied. Given this very conservative assumption, the Rand HIE study still indicated that free care would avert 106,000 deaths per year in the United States.[62]

A second study conducted by the Urban Institute suggested more modest gains, while confirming that the availability of medical care does yield significant reductions in death rates. Jack Hadley studied health and health spending for four hundred county groups in the United States. After correcting for confounding variables (age, race, sex, income, education, smoking), Hadley calculated that a 10 percent increase in health spending was associated with a 1.57 percent decrease in mortality rates. That relationship tended to hold steady across age, race, and sex groups.[63] Since the Rand HIE study found that free-care patients spent 14.6 percent more than the national average, Hadley's results suggest 47,000 deaths would be averted each year by free care.

Is there a contradiction between these statistics and the notion that universal coverage can actually lower system-wide medical costs? If the Rand HIE study found a 14.6 percent increase in health care costs, would not the provision of free medical care generate a 14.6 percent increase in the overall health care budget? Not at all. The Rand HIE actually measured increased charges to insurance companies, not the real cost of the increased care to hospitals, clinics, or doctor's offices.

Since the United States already has a surplus of medical facilities and personnel, it should not cost significantly more to expand care. In 1991, the average U.S. hospital had 177 beds, but only 117 were occupied. In addition to their own care, those 117 patients also paid the hospital's fixed costs, items such as building mortgages, heat, equipment, and round-the-clock staffing for laboratories. If hospital care increased by 14.6 percent under a National Health Program, it would not cause

14.6 percent more hospitals to be built. Rather, the number of occupied beds in the average hospital would rise from 117 to 134.6. Fixed costs would be spread over a larger number of patients, lowering the fixed cost per patient. The rise in total cost would be less than 14.6 percent. In economics terminology, the marginal cost of care is less than the average cost.

How much less is a matter of intense controversy within the medical industry. HMOs and other managed care plans negotiate discounts with hospitals in exchange for referring patients to otherwise empty beds. They haggle bitterly over this issue. Two older studies, one from the sixties and one from the seventies, estimated the marginal cost of hospital care at 55 and 74 percent of charges, respectively.[65] Thus, free care would cause a larger utilization increase than cost increase, most of which would be offset by administrative saving. However, universal access through a single-payer reform would not markedly increase net health care costs, a view substantiated by both the GAO and the CBO, the two principal research and investigative agencies of the U.S. Congress.[66]

Both the Clinton Administration and PNHP have proposed the creation of regional and national boards which would set practice guidelines and standards. But under the administration's proposal, physicians' work would be monitored not primarily by the boards but by officials of private insurance companies. In contrast the boards of an NHP would be publicly appointed or elected, and would set fees based on medical efficacy and overall cost containment at the national level, not the short-term pecuniary interests of an insurance company.

The National Health Plan boards, unlike Clinton's board, would also have the power to allocate capital investments, avoiding the excess supply of high technology services in the United States that not only drives up costs, but can drive down quality. For example, several studies have shown that surgical teams must perform a minimum number of specific complex procedures each year in order to maintain their professional competence. The American College of Surgeons has suggested guidelines for the minimum volume of such procedures that hospitals should perform annually.[67] However, more than a third of California's hospitals performing open heart surgery have dangerously low volumes, which raise both death rates and costs.

For transplants and several other complex surgical procedures, redundant facilities lead to lower levels of competence and adverse outcomes for patients.[68] Duplication raises costs because each hospital invests in expensive high technology equipment and maintains a full surgical team, which are underutilized. The Clinton Administration's plan proposed leaving decisions on capital investment in the hands of competing private institutions and thus would have failed completely to have halted the medical arms race.

By removing financial and bureaucratic obstacles to care and by encouraging care aimed at improving health and not at insurance companies' annual reports to shareholders, the single-payer system would unquestionably save tens of thousands of lives annually in the United States.

LONG-TERM CARE

In a health system deeply marred by racial, social, and economic inequalities, perhaps the most glaring disparity is the one between our ability to cure and our willingness to care. In the United States remarkable technical sophistication in the therapy of acute illness coexists with neglect for many of the disabled. Millions of Americans with disabilities cannot obtain the assistance that would enable them to live with maximum possible independence. The fortunate few with Medicaid or savings often find themselves in nursing homes that amount to little more than warehouses. In the home, family and friends care for the disabled unaided, uncompensated, and without respite.

Good long-term care (LTC) could ameliorate disability,

eliminate the costly substitution of acute for long-term care, prevent unnecessary nursing home placements, and provide a genuine safety net, both medical and financial, for people of all ages. The NHP would provide universal coverage for LTC through a public insurance program, pooling funds in existing public programs with new federal revenues raised through taxation. The financial risk should be spread across the entire population using a progressive financing system rather than compounding the misfortune of disability with the specter of financial ruin. Coverage should be universal, with access to services to be based on need rather than age, cause of disability, or income.

But LTC involves much more than just being able to see a doctor without financial barriers. The LTC component of the NHP would offer a continuum of medical and social services. This NHP would provide sheltered housing and assisted transportation designed to maximize functional independence. It would be coordinated with acute inpatient and ambulatory care. Private insurance companies have made only tentative efforts to market LTC insurance, and currently insure less than one percent of Americans.[69] This LTC insurance is unaffordable to most who need it, and rarely covers all necessary services.[70] Thus, about half of LTC expenses are paid out-of-pocket, with most of the remainder paid by Medicaid.[71] The financial burden for LTC falls most heavily on disabled members of the middle and working class who can qualify for Medicaid only after "spending down" their assets until they are impoverished.[72] Medicaid favors nursing home care by paying for it far more generously than for home or community-based services.

While an improvement over the current system, the Clinton LTC plan would still have maintained sharp inequalities. Average nursing home costs of $20,000 to $40,000 per year would bankrupt the majority of Americans within three years.[73] The level of cost-sharing envisioned by the Clinton proposals would have meant slower financial ruin, but ruin nonetheless. The Clinton plan included an option for states to give vouchers or lump-sum capitation payments to recipients, ratifying a two-tier system in which the affluent would pay extra to buy their way out of a bare bones public LTC program.

Most politicians have neglected the issue of LTC, and its needs are largely invisible to policy makers because the majority of services for disabled people—of any age—are provided by "informal" (unpaid) caregivers, mainly female family members, neighbors, or friends. More than 70 percent of those currently receiving LTC (3.2 million people) rely exclusively on unpaid caregivers; an additional 22 percent use both formal and informal care.[74] Of the more than 7 million informal care-givers, three-quarters are women, 35 percent are themselves over 65 years old, a third are in poor health, 10 percent have given up paid employment to assume the care of their loved one, and eight out of ten spend at least 4 hours every day providing care.[75] Such personal devotion can never be replaced by the assistance of even the kindest of strangers. It must be valued and supported, not supplanted by formal care.

Within the medical profession itself, LTC is neither well understood nor loved. Geriatric training is woefully underfunded.[76] Hence too few physicians are adequately equipped to address remediable medical problems that contribute to disability, while many are called on to assume responsibility for care that has more to do with personal maintenance and hygiene than with more familiar medical terrain.[77] Even when doctors know what should be done, the needed resources are often unavailable. The experts in providing care—nurses, homemakers, social workers, and the like—are often locked into a hierarchy which offers them little prestige for the important tasks they perform.

Total LTC costs (excluding "informal" services) amounted to at least $104 billion in 1990 (16 percent of total health spending).[78] Public programs, primarily Medicaid, financed about half of formal LTC. Consumers paid out-of-pocket for 40 percent of home services.[79] Private insurance paid less than 2 percent of nursing home costs.[80] Overall, a comprehensive LTC program would require $70 to $75.5 billion in new tax revenues, though two-thirds of this amount represents money currently spent privately that would be shifted onto the public ledger. Because LTC has been seriously underfunded, $18 to $23.5 billion in truly new spending ($100 to $130 per adult) would be needed to expand care and improve its quality.

These tax revenues could be raised from several sources: increasing the earned income tax credit for lower-income workers and removing the current ceiling on Social Security taxes would generate about $49 billion in additional revenue, while making such taxes less regressive.[81] A 10 percent surcharge on estates above $200,000 would raise $2 to 4 billion and taxing capital gains at death would raise about $5.5 billion.[82] The canard that the American people want something for nothing is often applied to LTC. Yet, polls have found that four out of five Americans support government action for a universal LTC and 75 percent would agree to increased taxes for LTC.[83]

The United States should borrow from the Canadian provinces of Manitoba and British Columbia, where LTC is a part of the basic health care entitlement regardless of age or income.[84] Case managers and specialists in needs assessment (largely nonphysicians) evaluate the need for LTC and authorize payment for services. Case management has allowed broad access to nursing home and community-based services without runaway inflation.

The NHP would cover all medically and socially necessary LTC services under a single public plan. Home health and support services as well as residential and institutional care would be included. In special circumstances, other services such as employment and training could be provided. Outreach and preventive services would be covered to minimize avoidable deterioration in functioning. Supportive housing environments, though essential for many who are frail and disabled, should be financed separately as part of housing rather than medical programs.

The NHP would consolidate all current federal and state

programs for LTC. At present eighty federal programs finance LTC services, including Medicare, Medicaid, the Veterans Administration, the Older Americans Act, and Title XX Social Services.[85] State disability insurance programs also finance some LTC. As with acute care, this myriad of programs leaves enormous gaps in both access and coverage, confuses consumers, and drives up administrative costs. In contrast, the proposed single-payer LTC program would be comprehensive, administratively spare, and "user friendly." Since most people needing LTC prefer to remain at home, services would promote independent living, using nursing homes as the last resort rather than as the primary approach to LTC [86]

With a federal mandate, each state would set up a network of local public LTC agencies. These local agencies would employ specialized panels of social workers, nurses, therapists, and physicians responsible for assessing individual needs, coordinating care, and, in some cases, delivering services. The agencies would certify eligibility for specific services, and assign a case manager when appropriate. Each state's LTC operating budget would be allocated to the local LTC agencies based on population, the number of elderly and disabled, the economic status of the population, case-mix, and cost of living. Each local LTC agency would apportion the available budget to cover the operating costs of approved providers in its community—though the actual payment apparatus would probably be centralized to avoid duplication of administrative functions.

Each institutional provider or community agency would negotiate a global operating budget with the local LTC agency. Physicians could be paid on a fee-for-service basis, or receive salaries from institutional providers. Providers participating in the public program would be required to accept the public payments as payment in full, and would not be allowed to charge patients directly for any covered service. Capital investment would be directed by state boards based on health planning goals.

Leaving LTC in the hands of profit-making companies

poses hazards to the nation's long-term health. At least 75 percent of the nursing homes and a growing proportion of home care agencies are operated by for-profit firms.[87] The vulnerable population needing LTC is often unable to prevent entrepreneurs from skimping on care in order to maximize profits.[88] The NHP would transform for-profit nursing homes into not-for-profits by paying owners a reasonable fixed rate of return on existing equity. New for-profit investment would be proscribed.

Coverage would extend to anyone, regardless of age or income, needing assistance with one or more activity of daily living (ADL) or instrumental activity of daily living (IADL). Local panels would have the flexibility, within their defined budgets, to authorize a wide range of services, taking into account such social factors as the availability of informal care. In all cases, programs should encourage independence and minimize professional intrusion into daily life. An estimated 3.6 percent (7.6 million persons) of the total noninstitutionalized population needs assistance with ADLs or IADLs.[89] Another 1.7 million people are institutionalized with physical or mental disabilities.[90] As with acute care, removing financial barriers will increase demand for formal services. LTC insurance could legitimately result in a 20 percent increase in nursing home utilization and a 50 to 100 percent increase in community and home health care use.[91] Those increases might be expected to level off after about three years, as occurred in Saskatchewan's program.[92]

Medicaid programs in several states have demonstrated that properly applied case management and utilization controls can both control costs and improve care by preventing unnecessary institutionalization, coordinating services, and assuring the use of the most appropriate care.[93] LTC must support and assist informal caregivers but informal caregivers should not be expected to undertake an overwhelming burden of care and must be offered support services, especially regular respite care.

Capitation (lump-sum advance payment) would be available to selected agencies. Two demonstrations using a capitated model to deliver acute and long-term care are the social health maintenance organizations (SHMOs), and the On Lok project in San Francisco, both highly successful.[94] Individual providers could also continue to operate on a contractual or fee-for-service basis.[95] In selected cases family members or other informal caregivers could be approved as providers. State LTC boards would award earmarked funds to local agencies offering the most promising proposals for innovation because innovation is particularly important for improving services to different age groups and disability categories.

No other segment of the health care system has as many documented quality problems as nursing homes, nearly one-third of which operate below minimum federal quality standards.[96] The NHP would pay only those LTC providers (including home care agencies) meeting uniform national quality standards. Earmarked funds would support urgently needed research to validate existing standards, and to develop new approaches to quality assurance.

Improving the training, wages, and morale of LTC workers is also crucial to quality. LTC workers currently earn 15–45 percent less than comparable hospital employees, and 20 percent of nursing home workers have no health insurance.[97] Nursing homes are not now required to provide around-the-clock RN care, few have specialized staff such as geriatric nurse practitioners, and aides are often inadequately trained. Many home care agencies have no professional staff or consultants. Wages in LTC organizations receiving payment from the NHP would be regulated to achieve parity with hospitals, with funding for this increase phased in over five years. Training and in-service education of LTC personnel and informal caregivers would also be funded. The nation needs to develop a cadre of physicians and nurses with special training in gerontology and geriatrics.[98]

By itself health care financing reform would only begin the process of creating a healthy society. Working together, physicians, social service providers, and LTC workers have the ability to ease suffering and assist the disabled to live with a maximum of independence and dignity. Our nation has the resources to provide better care for the disabled and elderly and it has a responsibility to develop a comprehensive single-payer LTC system. The public supports this type of approach. Health and human services professionals and public policy makers need the vision and courage to do it.

HEALTH CARE AND THE DEMOCRATIC PARTY

The election of Bill Clinton took place in the context of a twenty-year history of debate within the Democratic party over the elements of a successful presidential electoral strategy. Clinton was one of the principal organizers of the Democratic Leadership Council (DLC), the main caucus of the party's conservative wing. DLC analysts argued that the Democrats and the Republicans could each count on roughly 40 percent of the popular vote, and that presidential elections are fought over the 20 percent of the voters in the middle. These voters, known since 1980 as the Reagan Democrats, are presumed to be overwhelmingly white, culturally conservative, often racially prejudiced, and suspicious of activist government.

To court this segment of the electorate, DLC analysts maintained that the Democrats had to "move to the middle"; withdraw support from affirmative action; advocate a belligerent foreign policy; support the death penalty; and advocate new domestic programs only if they directly benefited the middle class or boosted employment. Furthermore, the ideologists of the DLC argued that the Democratic party had to abandon its "traditional hostility toward business," because the corporate economy is both the engine that drives the free enterprise economy and the cash cow for political campaigns.

The Democratic party's "progressive" wing, the descendent of Roosevelt's New Deal coalition, has advocated an alternative strategy. According to this view, the Democratic party can only regain and retain political hegemony through a program that would extend and deepen democracy. Until 1992, the turnout for presidential elections had declined progressively since 1964 and reached a low of 50 percent of the electorate. According to party progressives, a quiescent electorate could be mobilized through voter registration and turnout efforts and politicized by a genuine social democratic program. The elements of such a program would include: national health insurance; a diversion of spending from defense to the civilian infrastructure and education; and a shift in the tax burden to the wealthy.

Both voter turnout and identification with the Republican party increase as one travels up the income scale. Since marginal voters are traditionally Democratic, the progressives have argued that a winning strategy had to mobilize the marginal voter with a program that would appeal to the millions of lower- and middle-income citizens who usually do not vote. In 1992, Clinton cleverly mixed themes from both wings of the Democratic party. He obscured essentially conservative policies with populist rhetoric, and benefited from twelve years of public exhaustion and frustration with Reagan-Bush economic policies.

One of the Democratic party's crucial themes in its 1992 appeal to the electorate was health care reform. Clinton's health proposal is a microcosm of the DLC approach to social reforms. The entire managed competition approach was essentially an insurance industry proposal for reorganization, which would increase the insurer's dominance over health care. The Republicans abandoned the health care field during the 1992 campaign by confining their rhetoric largely to attacks on malpractice awards, hardly a clarion call for change. Predictably, legalistic tinkering with problems that account for less than one percent of the country's health care costs failed to capture the heart of the electorate.

By expressing sympathy with victims of the current health care system and by advocating reform, the Democrats were able to appeal to the underlying disquiet and palpable sense of economic crisis among middle- and working-class constituencies. The public face of the Clinton proposals was vague, while the insurance industry's ideological child—"managed competition"—became the centerpiece of Clinton's new reforms. The conservatives within the Democratic party thought their strategy successful. Health care reform had mobilized the electoral base, without antagonizing the business community.

However, the election might be seen as much as a vindication of the Democratic party's progressive strategy as of the DLC's. With a small surge in turnout, Clinton garnered only 43 percent of the popular vote; Clinton won the election not by winning the Reagan Democrats, but largely through support from the core Democratic constituencies. For all of his appeal to the center, Clinton merely split the coveted "center" among himself, Perot and Bush. When the dust had settled, the 1992 election offered no clear guide to a new campaign strategy in 1996. Nevertheless, the Clinton Administration continued the conservative DLC approach in its governing agenda, epitomized by Clinton's health reform proposals.

By embracing managed competition, Clinton precluded the cost saving only attainable through the establishment of a single-payer structure. The Clinton proposals ultimately sacrificed both universality and quality in order to keep the private insurance industry in the business of health care. In every society that combines universal coverage with effective cost containment, the private insurance industry has been barred from a commanding role in health care, and the profit motive has been minimized. Health care, like public education, has been made a nonprofit undertaking. Although the form has varied, the result in Germany, Britain, France, Sweden, Canada, and other nations with national health programs has been that the entire populations receive comprehensive coverage at a substantially lower percentage of the Gross National Product than in the "private" American insurance market. A similar solution is available to the United States

Advocates of a single-payer system introduced the American Health Security Act in the U.S. Congress. Within six months of its introduction, the number of cosponsors had grown from 53 to 89, one-fifth of the membership of the House. A broad coalition of citizens groups, consumer organizations, labor unions, and medical professionals have organized a national effort to establish a single-payer National Health Program.

A 1990 survey of health economists found that 52 percent favored Canadian-style reform, and more than half opposed an employer mandate.[99] Most important, the American people favor tax-financed national health insurance. A 1989 Harris poll found that 61 percent of Americans favored the Canadian system over the current U.S. system. A similar study of Canadian opinion found, by contrast, that 95 percent of Canadians favored their own system and only 3 percent would favor a shift to a U.S.-style system.[100] Survey after survey finds a majority of Americans in favor of tax-financed national health insurance.

Despite these majoritarian sentiments the Clinton Administration has repeatedly rejected single-payer proposals as "politically unfeasible," which has the effect of diminishing the support for such an approach. If Clinton had taken the lead and publicly defended the single-payer system, he could have consolidated this existing base of support and gone on to extend this base. The authors and other single-payer advocates have had a long-standing dialogue with members of the new Clinton Administration committed to some form of health care reform. Hillary Clinton and others have been willing to concede that the single-payer option is *the most rational proposal*. But Hillary Clinton rejected it as a viable option because she did not think the White House could overcome the influence of insurance and medical supply industries in the U.S. Congress. More to the point, she was unwilling to mount an effective challenge to these industries and mobilize the millions of Americans who are present or potential adversaries of these retrograde medical "special interest" groups. Tens of millions of dollars in PAC money have filled the campaign coffers of hundreds of congressional representatives, and these political markers were called in during the health care debate. Convinced from the start that they could not beat the powerful interests anchored in the insurance industry, the Clintons elected to join them by accepting a proposal the industry itself designed and called "reform." This was the essence of the Clinton's managed competition compromise, a Faustian bargain with insurers that would make future reform much harder to achieve.

In a conversation in the White House in February 1991 Hillary Clinton asked authors David Himmelstein and Steffie Woolhandler how the powerful insurance lobby within the U.S. Congress could possibly be defeated. We argued that strong presidential leadership backed by polls showing that 70 percent of Americans favor a tax-financed national health insurance system did offer a sound basis to do battle. Most Americans already support a tax-based system because they comprehend that a thousand-dollar tax is not more odious than a thousand-dollar insurance premium. Many understand that the $4,000 they now pay toward health care through insurance premiums, out of pocket medical expenses, and taxes (for Medicare, Medicaid, health benefits for teachers, the police, and politicians) could instead be funneled through a single-payer system and provide them with greater security and improved benefits. The popular foundation for a single-payer reform has existed for years. We argued that if this constituency were politically mobilized, grass-roots supporters could counter the PAC money and the political arm twisting of the insurance industry lobbyists. Our argument, however, was dismissed by Hillary Clinton as naive. She said, "Tell me something interesting, David."[101] Of course, what ultimately became interesting was how the Clintons' calculated compromise with the private insurance industry merely emboldened conservative opposition to any reform and led to an emasculation of their timid proposals in successive congressional committees.

Unfortunately, the decision of the Clintons to compromise fundamental principles and accept unprincipled bargains dictated by the insurance industry demobilized support for reform and assured an unsatisfactory outcome. Despite its rhetoric the Clinton compromise would have severely limited the choice of a doctor for most people. All but the wealthy would be forced to choose among cut-rate HMOs offering only a limited list of doctors. Moreover, the HMOs could fire doctors at will. (Colorado's largest HMO just terminated its contracts with three hundred orthopedists.) If your child's pediatrician were in a different plan from your gynecologist or orthopedist, your family would be forced to choose which relationship to disrupt. In Canada and throughout Western Europe such health care irrationalities do not exist. Canadians can see any doctor, anywhere in the country. A Canadian national health card entitles you to walk into any physician's office or hospital and receive care without being billed. When you pay your annual taxes, you have paid for your national health insurance coverage.

Moreover, the main cost containment strategy of the Clinton proposal—competition among HMOs—is irrelevant to the fifty percent of Americans who live in areas lacking the population density to support more than one "choice." A town's only hospital or HMO cannot compete with itself. But perhaps the real betrayals of reform are that millions of undocumented immigrants would remain uncovered; tens of millions who now have good coverage would be forced into stripped-down plans; and many would face crushing out-of-pocket costs for mental health and long-term care that the Clintons left mostly uncovered. The continued existence of such barriers to care are a direct consequence of the expensive compromise the Clintons made by adopting the insurance industry's design for reform. Universal, comprehensive coverage can only be afforded if the 11 percent of spending now wasted on unnecessary administrative costs and profits can be redirected to care by a single-payer plan.

The Clinton compromises have undermined the prospects for future reform. Their plan encouraged insurance company ownership of much of the health care system. At present, most hospitals and doctors are relatively independent, but they are being rapidly gobbled up by the insurer-owned HMOs that the Clintons are encouraging. We could convert to a single-payer system by diverting the money that currently flows through insurers to flow instead through the single-payer structure. But once the insurers have bought the hospitals (with our premium dollars) and employ the doctors and nurses, a single-payer reform will be more difficult. No doubt, we will pay twice, having to buy back from the insurers the health care system they have bought with our money.

Moreover, as cost savings failed to materialize from managed competition in the years ahead, wealthy Americans would inevitably question why they are paying high out-of-pocket costs for their coverage and substantial taxes to subsidize the lower-tier insurance for the poor. Calls for fiscal responsibility in Congress would once more lead to cuts in benefits for the working poor and unemployed. The Medicaid syndrome would be repeated as the poor and increasing numbers of the working class are pushed into ghettos of low-cost, low-quality HMOs. Care for the wealthy would be increasingly segregated in an elite tier with premiums and deductibles that few others could afford.

A single-payer system is not utopia, but it would avoid the most egregious disparities that now prevail, disparities that managed competition would exacerbate. The savings that are only possible through single-payer reform allow it to provide a universal system of high-quality coverage. It enlists the wealthy in assuring quality of care for all. In Canada, individuals from all classes have an interest in making the system work at the highest standards possible for all because every Canadian has the same insurer and access to the same hospitals and doctors.

By vesting each American with an equal share in the system, a single-payer reform could avoid multi-tiered care, while enhancing the commonweal.

The Washington health reform hoopla turned out to be a mere sideshow to the Clinton era's main event: the accelerating corporate takeover of health care. Patients' care and caregivers' working lives will be poorer in 1995 than in 1985, and this will be the case even if Congress manages to squeeze out a me-too variant of managed competition. The extinction of both professionalism and medical altruism, and the depersonalization of care, not the legislative details of a paltry reform, define the medical context for this decade.

When, early on, Clinton signaled that health care investors were safe on his watch—that for-profit HMOs, private insurers and other health care businesses would not just linger but flourish—he unleashed an unprecedented torrent of mergers and acquisitions. Never has control of so vast an industry shifted so rapidly from a dispersed array of small and medium-scale producers—in this case, doctors and local hospitals—to a few huge corporations whose leveraged financial clout is their only qualification for health care leadership.

Each week, thousands of physicians are forced into a bizarre variant of musical chairs: sell your practice on the terms offered, or be left out for good as your patients are herded into restrictive managed-care plans. In Springfield, Missouri, St. John's Hospital presented doctors with a deadline to sell out and sign on as employees of a new plan. Once doctors committed, their contracts called for $1,000-a-day penalty if they quit and practiced medicine within twenty-five miles of town.

The physicians' dilemma, in Springfield as elsewhere, is caused by the likely collapse of existing medical practice outside the realm of managed care. As we have previously discussed, HMOs typically employ one physician for every 800 enrollees, but the United States has one doctor for every 400 people. Hence HMO expansion absorbs many patients but relatively few physicians. When half the patients in a given region have signed on to managed care, only 250 patients per non-HMO physician remain, too few even to pay practice overhead. Congressional guarantees of free choice in a fee-for-service option are meaningless; market forces insure that non-HMO practice will shrivel, maintained only for an elite few able to afford astronomical fees. For most of us, the choice will be restricted to giant corporate HMO "A" or giant corporate HMO "B."

By 1993 ten firms controlled 70 percent of the HMO market; two of them, Met Life and Travellers, have since merged. Bowing to marketplace necessities, Blue Cross is going for-profit, so it can sell stock to raise the billions it needs to buy hospitals and clinics for its own managed care networks. Pharmaceutical giants Merck, SmithKline and Eli Lilly paid $13 billion in 1994 for firms that "manage" drug benefits, presaging the death of marketing through so-called drug detailing, whereby drug companies provide free trinkets and intensive miseducation to individual physicians. In its place: drug choices made directly by subsidiaries of the drug makers, with sales commissions (a. k. a. bribes) for pharmacists who lure patients to the desired brand.

The top ten for-profit hospital chains have been coupling like rabbits (though, unlike rabbits, each liaison leaves fewer firms, not more). In September 1993 Columbia swallowed Galen; in February HCA; in July, it proposed the takeover of Medical Care America. Quorum acquired part of Charter in October 1993, growing to 32,000 beds. American Healthcare Management and Ornda merged in April 1994. Healthtrust bought Epic in May. And in most big cities, the non-chain hospitals are consolidating into a few giant groups. Under the guise of competition we have galloped toward oligopoly.[102]

Meanwhile, as Congress debated coverage for the uninsured, the care of the insured was being transformed. The patient/doctor relationship is giving way to the employer/health plan contract. Managed care plans often force physicians and therapists to consult the plan's "utilization reviewers" (the insurers' representatives assigned to cut costs by limiting care) before discussing therapy with the patient, and then forbid disclosure of compromises on quality.[103] General Electric employees in Boston are now forbidden to call their doctors for an appointment; instead, they must call a company reviewer, who filters requests. In California, Kaiser has told its primary care doctors that their patient caseloads have been increased to 2,000, more than double the prevailing HMO ratio. The seven-minute doctor's visit becomes the norm, while health planners fret that there will soon be 165,000 unemployed doctors. Health plan administrators demand industrial "efficiency" at the level of each doctor/patient encounter, producing chaotic inefficiency for the health care system as a whole.

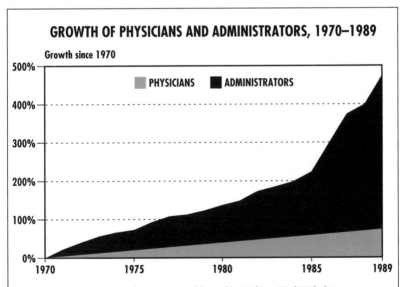

GROWTH OF PHYSICIANS AND ADMINISTRATORS, 1970–1989

Source: Bureau of the Census, *Statistical Abstract of the United States*, 102nd–109th editions (Washington: Government Printing Office, 1981–90)

There has been considerable discussion of the growing surplus of physicians in the United States, but little discussion of the surplus of bureaucrats. In fact, administrators are the most rapidly growing segment of the health care labor force. Between 1970 and 1989 the number of health care administrators in the United States increased almost six-fold, while the number of physicians (and other clinical personnel) doubled. It apparently takes substantial administrative effort and expense to keep sick patients out of empty hospital beds.

The new health care powers know finance, insurance, perhaps law—not medicine, or nursing, or cleaning bed pans, or patienthood. The new structure of care aims at profit, its new leaders are experts in that field. Why should doctors and nurses manage care; do chefs run McDonalds?

The Washington process that produced the Clintons' health plan is emblematic of the new structure. The policy experts and health management leaders have no medical or nursing knowledge, no clinical experience, no intimate encounter with illness. Hillary Rodham Clinton's task force of 500 included only a handful of people who had ever been to a hospital ward outside visiting hours; most were too young and healthy even to have served as patients. It is no wonder they followed a script written by the Jackson Hole Group—a ménage funded by insurers, convened by Nixon's health policy guru, Paul Ellwood, and guided by Alain Enthoven, Robert MacNamara's Pentagon protégé who went on to a senior position at the military-contracting Litton Industries before sinking his teeth into health policy. The result, as Ellwood forecast: conversion to larger units of production, substitution of capital for labor, and "profitability as the mandatory condition of survival"—a nightmare vision of for-profit, corporate medicine, utterly indifferent to the human experience of care.

For its part, the AMA, having long ago abandoned patients' interest, has been so distracted by its fear of government that it barely noticed insurance company shackles snapping shut on its profession. The surgeons, quick to clamp a bleeder, were the first in organized medicine to react. The 63,000-member American College of Surgeons endorsed a single-payer system; it is the only way to preserve their autonomy, and even jobs, as managed care plans whittle their specialist rosters. The conservative surgeons are strange but welcome bedfellows for the progressive doctors who rallied 6,000 strong to Physicians for a National Health Program, the Chicago-based group that put single-payer on the American medical map in 1989.

The legislative details of whatever emerges from the years of sterile Congressional debate will fade to insignificance. The essential truths will continue to be self-evident. Tens of millions will remain uninsured as promised savings from competition and managed care evaporate, and as government subsidies fall prey to budget-cutting. In Massachusetts (which is a world leader in both HMO membership and health costs) more people are uninsured today than when Governor Michael Dukakis's "pay-or-play" plan, with its employer mandates became law in 1988. Like the Democrats' 1994 versions, Massachusetts' universal health care bill coupled a rosy promise of future coverage with a green light to health care corporations. As costs soared, universality was indefinitely delayed.

As in Massachusetts, Congress's promises of full coverage are ephemeral, but the corporate advance toward a medical system dominated by a few giant, vertically integrated firms continues apace. Insurers will own hospitals, surgicenters, and home care agencies; employ doctors and the rest of the medical work force; and perhaps merge with drug firms. For the insured, care will be defined by a deal struck between a corporate care purchaser (i.e. your employer) and a corporate deliverer. In such a context, whither real health care reform?

In many areas of the country small-scale, fee-for-service practice is already dead or dying, foreclosing a purely Canadian style reform for America. Once most doctors have become HMO and hospital employees, breaking up these institutional arrangements would severely disrupt care. Resurrecting the Atlantis of mid-twentieth-century medicine may be impossible.

Therefore, an anticorporate, antimarket focus for reform is ever more germane. Corporate competitive imperatives are the palpable force destroying care. The managers and financiers who increasingly dominate care are not bad people (if so, we would need only replace them); they are just responding appropriately to a system that demands misbehavior: put profits before patients or go under.

Mere opposition to corporate HMOs is insufficient: we must devise their transformation. We need control by patients and caregivers, not stockholders, managers, and employers. We need medical integration, so that health care in communities is not carved up among ostensibly competing organizations, each avoiding financially unrewarding tasks and patients, and shunning community-wide cooperation. We must scale care to a human size, so patients and providers can know one another and receive the care that is needed, not act as interchangeable corporate cogs. Unless HMO physicians, workers, and patients are centrally involved in planning this transformation, and in the movement for reform, it will surely fail. Recapturing the rational service orientation that characterized the original pre-paid group practices (e.g., Group Health Cooperative of Puget Sound, a consumer-controlled cooperative, and even the early Kaiser, with its altruistic leadership and physician corps) can be revitalizing.

A public single-payer system can evolve from HMOs and corporate care—if there is sufficient political pressure from a mass movement. Such a reform may share features with a national health service—salaried practice in integrated systems of care, with accountability to an electorate rather than to a corporate bureaucracy shaped by market forces.

A ROAD WELL TRAVELED

The United States is at a crossroads in domestic policy. In terms of its health policy, the United States could catch up with the rest of the advanced industrial world. It is still an open question whether it will or not. In the late 1940s, the United States wrestled with National Health Insurance; at the same time Great Britain adopted a National Health Service and Canada began its march toward national health insurance. The parallel experiences of the three countries in the aftermath of the Second World War are instructive.

In the midst of the Second World War a coalition government of national unity was formed in Britain, which brought together Conservative, Labor, and Liberal parties. When the Labor party joined the coalition, it pressed Winston Churchill and his Conservative party to make some offer to British workers and their families that would hold forth the prospect of a better postwar society, a vision of a Britain worth fighting for. These discussions resulted in a special commission chaired by the Liberal peer, Lord William Beveridge, which released a report in 1942 outlining a plan for restructuring British society. It was a stinging critique of inequality in the United Kingdom. Perhaps its most prominent recommendation was the establishment of a National Health Service. As the war drew to a close, Conservative Health Minister Henry Willink took the first tentative steps toward reform of Britain's health care system.

But the British electorate, viewing the Labor Party as more committed to the new society envisioned in the Beveridge Report, swept Labor to its first unchallenged majority in the House of Commons in the postwar elections. In 1947, Parliament passed the National Health Service Act, crafted by Labor's Minister of Health Aneurin Bevan, a fiery Welsh socialist. Bevan devised a more sweeping reform than Beveridge had proposed, including nationalization of British hospitals.

The National Health Service was vociferously opposed by the British Medical Association (BMA). Bevan negotiated exhaustively with the BMA on a number of critical issues—many of them conceded earlier by Willink—including abolishing Britain's system of exclusive private practice, and incorporating private and charitable hospitals into the service. British doctors feared that the system would make them civil servants and would curtail drastically both their clinical freedom and their incomes. Bevan had indeed proposed a minimal annual salary to keep young doctors afloat as they built their practices but this was a far cry from making them civil servants.

The BMA conducted a plebiscite of its members just three months before the National Health System Act went into effect on July 5, 1948. Bevan's introduction of an amendment to permit doctors the choice of rejecting the salary and taking all their income from fees took some of the sting out of the opposition brewing in the medical community. Nevertheless, a majority of general practitioners voting in the plebiscite indicated that they would not join the new service. Newspapers predicted that many British citizens would refuse to join the National Health Service.

On July 5, three-quarters of Britain's population signed up. By the end of the year 97 percent had joined. The opposition expressed in the BMA plebiscite dissolved almost immediately as 90 percent of Britain's general practitioners participated almost from the start.[104] Churchill's Conservatives, who had nominally pledged to create a national health system when in power, voted against the National Health Service Act. Within five years, however, the Tories were claiming the success of the National Health Service as their own, derived from the Beveridge Report and the efforts of the wartime Conservative government. A seemingly radical social program rapidly won over its conservative opposition once it was implemented, because it was universal, effective, and popular.

In Saskatchewan, Canada, Tommy Douglas led the Commonwealth Cooperative Federation, an agrarian socialist party that gained a majority in the province's parliament in 1944. Douglas had suffered a severe leg injury as a child in rural Saskatchewan, and the local doctor saw no hope of avoiding amputation. But Douglas' father had the resources to bring him to a big city hospital, where the leg was saved. Gaining a parliamentary majority, Douglas vowed that no child should be denied the kind of care that had been so important to him. To emphasize his commitment to health, he became not only the provincial prime minister, but also its minister of health. His party proposed a national health insurance program very similar to that proposed by President Truman in 1948. The first part of the plan, introduced in 1947, covered hospital care, but Saskatchewan's doctors successfully blocked the proposal to extend the coverage to pay doctor's bills. The hospital plan worked well, and spread nationwide, with the national government agreeing to pick up part of each province's costs. By 1960, Douglas was prepared to take on the doctors, and called an election to affirm a mandate to proceed with extending coverage to include physician services, and he won.

The Saskatchewan plan was greeted by a bitter physicians' strike that was ultimately defeated with the assistance of progressive doctors from the United States and the United Kingdom who came to Saskatchewan to help fill the gaps. Again Saskatchewan's initiative proved successful. When the Conservative national government appointed Chief Justice Emmett Hall of Canada's Supreme Court to chair a commission to recommend changes in health care in Canada, Hall's commission advocated nationwide adoption of the Saskatchewan model. Despite an acrimonious parliamentary debate, the resulting bill was passed in 1966 by an extraordinary 177 to 2 majority—few members of parliament were willing publicly to oppose national health insurance. Physicians soon learned to live with the plan, and even love it. Polls show that two-thirds of Canadian physicians prefer their system to the U.S.-style system they used to have, and most are happy in their practices and would urge their child to become a doctor. More important, the vast majority of Canadians support the plan, and no Canadian political party advocates abolishing it.

Events broke somewhat differently south of the border. The year after Saskatchewan's hospital plan was implemented, and the same year that the British National Health Service was established, Harry Truman made national health insurance a centerpiece of his upset victory in the U.S. presidential election. The next year, Truman took the fight into Congress. The AMA routed Truman's reform efforts with a campaign that would become a model for high-stakes Washington lobbying in the decades to come. Congressional campaign coffers were stuffed with cash and the AMA turned national health insurance into its own variant of the "red menace."

Truman operated without the benefit of the British and Canadian parliamentary systems, which give a majority party virtually unchecked power to legislate its program. But he also lacked the profound consensus established in Britain during the war, as embodied in the Beveridge Commission, or in Saskatchewan. As a result, organized medicine and conservative business interests destroyed national health insurance, leaving entrenched employment-based private insurance as the primary financing mechanism for American health care. Ever vigilant against "socialized medicine," the AMA fought Medicare throughout the fifties and sixties. Yet, much like the BMA, the AMA's objections to Medicare and Medicaid rapidly evaporated upon implementation of the programs. Nevertheless, most doctors still vehemently opposed national health insurance for the American people as a whole.

During the 1970s and 1980s American physicians began to see insurance firms turn from an unobtrusive silent partner that just paid the bills to a powerful independent force that increasingly dictated practice and hassled doctors. The old bugaboo of "rationed medicine" that would intrude in the examining room and limit clinical freedom was gradually coming true. However, the culprit was not the government, but insurance companies.

Responding to the growing threat that insurers would take over medicine, a quiet consensus emerged among doctors for some sort of national health insurance, although most underestimated their colleagues' willingness to change. A 1986 survey of physicians found that 56 percent of doctors favored some form of national health insurance. But 74 percent said they thought most of their colleagues oppose national health insurance.[105]

In 1986 a group of physicians, most of them veterans of the 1960s civil rights and peace movements, met at a conference in New Hampshire and agreed that the time was right to approach colleagues with a proposal for a Canadian-style health care reform, and they formed Physicians for a National Health

Program. When the prestigious *New England Journal of Medicine* published the group's manifesto, thousands of physicians joined the campaign, and the national press took notice. The growing discontent with insurance company bullying, oppressive paperwork, and inability to get good care for their patients has led a large portion of the medical profession to embrace a single-payer reform. While the AMA has held fast in opposition, the sixty-thousand-member American College of Surgeons has endorsed the single-payer system, along with the National Medical Association (the organization of African-American physicians), the American Medical Women's Association, and many others.

Today, when one tallies the balance sheet of potential political support for a single-payer system, the outlines of a huge coalition emerge. First, there are the 38.9 million uninsured Americans who would clearly support the plan. To this number add the tens of millions of underinsured, including elderly Americans for whom a single-payer plan would dramatically improve coverage and the tens of millions of HMO members who bridle at the restrictions on their care. Medicaid recipients would find themselves with the same benefits as everyone else, removing the twin burdens of substandard care and the stigma of welfare. Big business, while wary of government social spending, might accede to a single-payer system because it could control their costs. Though the NHP would convert corporate health premiums into corporate health taxes, total corporate health spending would stabilize. Unions that have watched health costs eat up wages for more than a decade would find themselves in a position to bargain for wage increases again.

While many providers still resist a single-payer option, even formal opposition from the AMA may ultimately be reversed when the full implications of the managed competition alternative become clearer to them. Small businesses not currently offering health benefits and the insurance industry will remain prime opponents of a single-payer system. The

National Federation of Independent Businesses stridently opposed the employer mandate provisions of the Clinton proposal, suggesting that any plan requiring taxes or payments by small businesses would be fought.

This leaves the insurance industry, which more than any other force has used its powers and influence to strangle a genuine reform of the American health care system. Since a single-payer system would outlaw private insurance for most health benefits, there is no squaring the political circle. The insurance industry must be beaten head on. The Clintons' populist rhetoric always was hollow because their proposal would end ultimately with the entrenchment and dominance by the giants in the insurance industry. A genuine popular crusade against private insurers could draw upon the deep well of potential public support for a single-payer system. Effectively mobilized, a popular coalition could sweep aside the insurance industry's PAC money and lobbying efforts. In the grand tradition of Social Security, the single-payer option represents a potentially powerful political agenda with winning politics at its core.

Unlike Britain after the Great Depression and the Second World War, when the Labor party rallied the British electorate's profound desire for social changes, the United States is not experiencing a political sea change. Nevertheless, broad political consensus has developed that American health care is in crisis and the experiences of other countries present a powerful argument in favor of the single-payer option. The reform proposals of the Clinton administration could never have achieved their stated goals. As the GAO and the CBO have independently made clear, only the single-payer system can accomplish the goals of quality care and universal coverage on a sound financial basis.

Wedded as they were to managed competition, the Clintons could never resolve the contradiction between improved access and affordability. When the numbers did not add up, their only choice was to abandon universal coverage. Since they refused to confront and defeat the insurance industry, they were ultimately driven into a sequence of compromises and half-measures that could not deliver the goods. And their false pragmatism may well have dashed the hopes of a generation for genuine health care reform.

The struggle over health care's future will continue. The declining standard of care and caring touches a widening circle of patients, doctors, and other health workers, including groups that have been quite powerful until recently. Top-class care will be reserved for an ever smaller aristocracy, with 98 percent of us relegated to factory-style medicine or worse. Even the local elites that have heretofore controlled local hospitals will be force-fed bitter pills, as national hospital chains and managed care plans take over. The constituency for opposition will necessarily broaden.

The strength of the single-payer movement has been and must remain a clear vision of health care that is kind to patients, satisfying for caregivers, and fiscally conservative. In contrast, Clinton's plan, even before all the compromises, was a prescription for corporate takeover. Few could, or should, rally to this banner. Clinton did not try and fail. He refused to try.

A dark outcome is not inevitable. An aroused and well-informed public can push genuine reform forward. Any battle fought on the higher ground of genuine concern for health ultimately favors a single-payer system. A solution based on "managed competition" requires a trillion-dollar leap of faith across a chasm littered with the proven failures of its constituent parts: HMOs do not control costs and employer mandates do not produce universal access. Meanwhile, for nearly half a century, Western European and Canadian single-payer systems have provided quality health care to every citizen at affordable costs. We do not need to reinvent the wheel to reform health care. But we do need to defeat an insurance industry that would deny us the rational solution that would finally bring health security and safety to the people of this country.

Notes

1 "Dole: Nation Has Health Care Problems, But No Health Care Crisis," *Washington Post,* January 26, 1994.

2. David Himmelstein and Steffie Woolhandler, *The National Health Program Chartbook* (Cambridge: Center for National Health Program Studies/ Harvard Medical School, 1992), p. 79.

3. John Canham-Clyne, "Health Care Reform: Pay or Play," *Pacifica National Radio News,* March 2, 1993.

4. *Sources of Health Insurance and Characteristics of the Uninsured: Analysis of the March 1993 Current Population Survey* (Washington: Employee Benefit Research Institute, Issue Brief No. 145, January 1994), p. 5.

5. Himmelstein and Woolhandler, *Chartbook,* p. 27.

6. Ibid.

7. "Clinton Address: We Can No Longer Afford to Ignore What is Wrong," *Washington Post,* September 23, 1993.

8. Himmelstein and Woolhandler, *Chartbook,* p. 79. Only three percent of Canadians say that they would trade their health system for what exists in the United States. See Robert J. Blendon, "Three Systems: A Comparative Survey," *Health Management Quarterly I* (1989), 2-10.

9. D. Himmelstein, S. Woolhandler, and the Writing Committee of the Working Group on Program Design, "A National Health Program for the United States: A Physician's Proposal," *New England Journal of Medicine* 320 (1989), 102-08. See also K. Grumbach, T. Bodenheimer, D. Himmelstein, and S. Woolhandler, "Liberal Benefits, Conservative Spending: The

Physicians for a National Health Program Proposal," *Journal of the American Medical Association (JAMA)* 265:19 (1991), 2549-54.

10. 103rd Congress, Bill H.R. 1200 and S. 491, "The American Health Security Act of 1993."

11. M. L. Brown, L. G. Kessler, and F. G. Reuter, "Is the Supply of Mammography Machines Outstripping Need and Demand? An Economic Analysis," *Annals of Internal Medicine* 113 (1990), 547; Himmelstein and Woolhandler, *Chartbook*, p. 59.

12. United States General Accounting Office, *Canadian Health Insurance: Lessons for the United States* (Washington: GAO, June 1991), p. 7.

13. S. Woolhandler, D. Himmelstein, J. Lewontin, "Administrative Costs in U.S. Hospitals," *New England Journal of Medicine* 329 (1993), 400-03.

14. GAO, *Canadian Health Insurance*, p. 6.

15. Congressional Budget Office, *American Health Security Act of 1993: H.R. 1200* (Washington: CBO, December 16, 1993), table 2, p. 9.

16. Himmelstein and Woolhandler, *Chartbook*, p. 79.

17. Woolhandler et al., "Administrative Costs."

18. "Clinton Address: We Can No Longer Afford."

19. Associated Press, "Hawaii Health Care Is Called Model for U.S.," *New York Times*, May 19, 1993.

20. D. Himmelstein, S. Woolhandler, I. Hellander, J. Moloo, S. Wolfe, *The Growing Epidemic Uninsurance: New Data on the Health Insurance Coverage of Americans* (Cambridge: Center for National Health Program Studies/ Harvard Medical School, 1994).

21. A. Enthoven and R. Kronick, "A Consumer-Choice Health Plan for the 1990s: Universal Health Insurance in a System Designed to Promote Quality and Economy," *New England Journal of Medicine* 320 (1989), 29-37, 94-101.

22. Robin Toner, "Hillary Clinton's Potent Brain Trust on Health Care Reform," *New York Times,* February 28, 1993.

23. Enthoven and Kronick, "A Consumer-Choice Health Plan."

24. "Clinton Address: We Can No Longer Afford."

25. Lawrence D. Brown, *Politics and Health Care Organization: HMOs as Federal Policy* (Washington: Brookings Institution, 1983), p. 140.

26. Woolhandler et al., "Administrative Costs," p. 400.

27. John Canham-Clyne, "Health Care Reform: Managed Competition," *Pacifica National Radio News,* March 4, 1994.

28. V. R. Fuchs, T. S. Hahn, "How Does Canada Do It? A Comparison of Expenditures for Physicians' Services in the United States and Canada," *New England Journal of Medicine* 323 (1990), 884-90. See also Himmelstein and Woolhandler, *Chartbook*, p. 68.

29. U.S. Bureau of the Census, *Workers with Low Earnings: 1964-1990* (Washington: U.S. Government Printing Office [GPO], 1992).

30. Himmelstein and Woolhandler, *Chartbook,* p. 38.

31. "Sources of Health Insurance and Characteristics of the Uninsured," p. 30.

32. Himmelstein and Woolhandler, *Chartbook,* p. 15.

33. "Health Security Act," *Congressional Record* 139:148 (October 28, 1993), pp. E-2580-81.

34. CBO, *American Health Security Act.* The CBO calculates that overall administrative costs under H.R. 1200 would fall to 3.5 percent of health expenditures by the year 2000, and hold steady thereafter. However, "Medicare's administrative cost rate is about 2 percent, and the administrative cost of Canada's single-payer system is less than 2 percent of spending. Although the administrative costs of the national health insurance program might eventually fall closer to the Canadian level, the estimate assumes that this level would not be reached within the first seven years." See p. 7.

35. Ibid., p. 4.

36. S. Woolhandler and D. Himmelstein, "Socialized Medicine is Good Business," *In These Times,* January 25, 1992. For methodology see S. Woolhandler and D. Himmelstein, "The Deteriorating Administrative Efficiency of the U.S. Health Care System," *New England Journal of Medicine* 324 (1991), 1253-54.

37. Ibid.

38. Woolhandler et al., "Administrative Costs," p. 401.

39. Woolhandler and Himmelstein, "Socialized Medicine is Good Business." Authors' personal communication with Giles Fortin and Lothar W. Rehmer, Health Information Division, Ministry of Health and Welfare, Canada.

40. Ibid. As noted in this article, "At one Northeastern teaching hospital, the proportion of total expenditures devoted to administration has doubled over the past five years."

41. GAO, *Canadian Health Insurance,* p. 63. In footnote 2 of the GAO report the authors estimate $706.9 billion of estimated health care expenditures for 1991. GAO estimates $67 billion in administrative savings which equal 9 percent of total expenditures.

42. Jane Fritsch, "Empire Blue Cross Gave False Report to '92 Legislature," *New York Times,* June 18, 1993.

43. GAO, *Employer Based Insurance: High Costs, Wide Variation Threaten System,* (Washington: GAO, September 1992), p. 7.

44. "Clinton Address: We Can No Longer Afford."

45. GAO, *Canadian Health Insurance,* pp. 53-61.

46. Ibid., p. 83.

47. D. P. Andrulis, A. Kellerman, E. Z. Hintz, and B. B. Hackman, "Emergency Departments and Crowding in United States Teaching Hospitals," *Annals of Emergency Medicine* 20 (1991), 980.

48. S. H. Rowley, "Prescription from Canada: Would Universal Health Care Work in this Country?" *Chicago Tribune Sunday Magazine,* May 31, 1992.

49. M. M. Bortin, M. M. Horowitz, and A. A. Rimm, "Increasing Utilization of Allogenic Bone Marrow Transplantation: Results of the 1988-1990 Survey," *Annals of Internal Medicine* 116 (1993), 507.

50. J. Gabel, H. Cohen, and S. Fink, "Americans' Views on Health Care: Foolish Inconsistencies?" *Health Affairs* 8:1 (1989), 111.

51. R. A. Hayward, M. F. Shapiro, H. E. Freedman, and C. R. Corey, "Inequities in Health Services among Insured Americans: Do Working Age Adults Have Less Access to Medical Care than the Elderly?" *New England Journal of Medicine* 318 (1988), 1507.

52. J. S. Weissman, R. Stern, S. Fielding, and A. M. Epstein, "Delayed Access to Health Care: Risk Factors, Reasons, and Consequences," *Annals of Internal Medicine* 114 (1991), 326.

53. C. M. Winslow, J. Kosecoff, M. R. Chassin, D. E. Kanouse, and R. H. Brook, "The Appropriateness of Performing Coronary Artery Bypass Graft Surgery," *JAMA* 260: *505;* C. M. Winslow, D. H. Solomon, M. R. Chassin, J. Kosecoff, N. J. Merrick, and R. H. Brook, "The Appropriateness of Carotid Endarterectomy," *New England Journal of Medicine* 318 (1988), 721.

54. Blendon, "Three Systems."

55. J. E. Ware, Jr., R. H. Brook, W. H. Rogers, E. B. Keeler, A. Ross Davies, K. Donald Sherbourne, G. A. Goldberg, P. Camp, and J. P. Newhouse, "Comparison of Health Outcomes at a Health Maintenance Organization with Those of C-4 Services," *The Lancet* 1 (1986), 1017.

56. Glenn Kramon, "Insurers Move to the Front Lines Against Rising Health Care Costs," *New York Times,* August 25, 1991.

57. Woolhandler and Himmelstein, "Socialized Medicine is Good Business."

58. "Malpractice: A Straw Man—The 'Crisis' that Isn't," *Consumer Reports,* July 1993, p. 443. According to the analysis by *Consumer Reports,* "The U.S. Department of Health and Human Services puts the total cost of malpractice at less than 1 percent of total health outlays."

59. Martin L. Gonzalez, ed., *Socio-Economic Characteristics of Medical Practice* (Chicago: American Medical Association, 1994).

60. T. A. Brennan, L. L. Leape, N. M. Laird, L. Herbert, A. R. Localio, A. G. Lawthers, J. P. Newhouse, P. C. Weiler, and H. H. Hiatt, "Incidence of Adverse Events and Negligence in Hospitalized Patients:

Results of the Harvard Medical Practice Study I," *New England Journal of Medicine* 324 (1991), 370-76.

61. R. H. Brook, J. E. Ware, Jr., W. H. Rogers et al., "Does Free Care Improve Adults' Health? Results from a Randomized Controlled Trial," *New England Journal of Medicine* 309 (1983), 1426-34. See also J. P. Newhouse, W. G. Manning, C. N. Morris et al., "Some Interim Results from a Controlled Trial of Cost Sharing in Health Insurance," *New England Journal of Medicine* 305 (1981), 1501-07; E. B. Keeler, R. H. Brook, G. A. Goldberg et al., "How Free Care Reduced Hypertension in the Health Insurance Experiment," *JAMA* 254 (1985), 1926-31.

62. S. Woolhandler and D. Himmelstein, "Free Care: A Quantitative Analysis of Health and Cost Effects of a National Health Program for the United States," *International Journal of Health Services* 18:3 (1988), 393-99.

63. J. Hadley, *More Medical Care, Better Health?* (Washington: The Urban Institute, 1982), p. 162 .

64. Woolhandler and Himmelstein, "Socialized Medicine Is Good Business." See also Woolhandler and Himmelstein, "Free Care: A Quantitative Analysis," p. 221.

65. Woolhandler and Himmelstein, "Free Care: A Quantitative Analysis," p. 221.

66. GAO, *Canadian Health Insurance*, p. 7, and CBO, *American Health Security Act*, p. 9.

67. Unlike the AMA, the American College of Surgeons has publicly declared itself in favor of a single-payer system. Sharon McGrath, "Surgeons Back Single-Payer: ACS Says National Plan Would Protect Patients' Choice of Doctors," *American Medical News,* February 28, 1994.

68. Woolhandler and Himmelstein, *Chartbook*, p. 57. A. C. Enthoven, "What Can Europeans Learn from Americans," *Health Care Financing Review, Annual Supplement,* 1989, p. 49. H. S. Luft, J. P. Bunker, and A. C. Enthoven, "Should Operations Be Regionalized? The Empirical Relation Between Surgical Volume and Mortality," *New England Journal of Medicine* 301 (1979), 1364.

69. U.S. Bipartisan Commission on Comprehensive Health Care, *A Call For Action: Final Report* (Washington: GPO, 1990).

70. R. M. Ball and T. N. Bethell, *Because We're All in This Together: The Case for a National Long-Term Care Insurance Policy* (Washington: Families U.S.A. Foundation, 1989); J. Firman, W. Weissert, and C. E. Wilson, *Private Long-Term Care Insurance: How Well Is It Meeting Consumer Needs and Public Policy Concerns?* (Washington: United Seniors Health Cooperative, 1988); C. L. Estes, *Long Term Care: Requiem for Commercial Private Insurance* (San Francisco: Institute for Health and Aging, 1990).

71. U.S. House Select Committee on Aging, *Private Long-Term Care*

Insurance: Unfit for Sale? A Report by the Chairman of the Subcommittee on Health and Long-Term Care (Washington: GPO, 1989).

72. *InterStudy's Long-Term Care Expansion Program: A Proposal for Reform* (Excelsior, Minn.: InterStudy, 1988).

73. R. L. Associates, *The American Public Views Long-Term Care: A Survey Conducted for the American Association of Retired Persons and the Villers Foundation* (Princeton: R.L. Associates, 1987).

74. K. Liu, K. G. Manton, and B. M. Liu, "Home Care Expenses for the Disabled Elderly," *Health Care Review* 7 (1985), 51-57; R. Stone, R. G. L. Cafferata, and J. Sangl, "Caregivers of the Frail Elderly: A National Profile," *Gerontologist* 27 (1987), 616-26; U.S. Senate, *Developments in Aging* (Washington: GPO, 1989); U.S. Senate, *A Report of the Special Committee on Aging* (Washington: GPO, 1989); R. Stone, *Aging in the Eighties: Age 65 Years and Over—Use of Community Services* (NCHS Advance Data, 1986).

75. Liu, Manton, Liu. "Home Care Expenses."

76. W. R. Hazzard, "A Report Card on Academic Geriatrics in 1991: A Struggle for Academic Respectability," *Annals of Internal Medicine* 115 (1991), 229-30.

77. J. W. Rowe, E. Drossman, and E. Bond, "Academic Geriatrics for the Year 2000," Institute of Medicine Report, *New England Journal of Medicine* 316 (1987), 1425-28; R. Kane, D. Solomon, J. Beck, E. Keeler, and R. Kane, "The Future Need for Geriatric Manpower in the U.S.," *New England Journal of Medicine* 302 (1980), 1327-32.

78. U.S. Department of Commerce (DOC), International Trade Administration, *Health and Medical Services: U.S. Industrial Outlook 1990* (Washington: DOC, 1990).

79. R. J. Price and C. O'Shaughnessy, *Long-Term Care for the Elderly,* Congressional Research Service Issue Brief (Washington: The Library of Congress, 1990).

80. CBO, *Statement of Nancy Gordon, Assistant Director for Human Resources and Community Department before the Health Task Force Committee on the Budget, U.S. House of Representatives* (Washington: CBO, October 1, 1987); U.S. Department of Health and Human Services (DHHS), *Task Force on Long-Term Care Policies, Report to Congress and the Secretary: Long-Term Health Care Policies* (Washington: GPO, 1987); Division of National Cost Estimates (DNCE), Office of the Actuary, Health Care Financing Administration, "National Health Expenditures, 1986–2000," *HCFA* 8 (1987), 1-36; K. R. Leit and M. S. Freedland, "National Medical Care Spending," *Health Affairs* 7 (1988), 124-36.

81. D. Blumenthal, M. Schlesinger, and P. B. Drumbeller, *Renewing the Promise: Medicare and Its Reform* (New York: Oxford University Press, 1988).

82. U.S. Bipartisan Commission on Comprehensive Health Care, *A Call for Action: Final Report* (Washington, September 1990).

83. R. L. Associates, *The American Public Views Long-Term Care;* Louis Harris, *Majorities Favor Passage of Long-Term Health Care Legislation* (New York: Louis Harris & Associates, March 13, 1988).

84. R. L. Kane and R. A. Kane, *A Will and a Way: What the United States Can Learn from Canada about Caring for the Elderly* (New York: Columbia University Press, 1985).

85. U.S. Senate, *Developments in Aging.*

86. A. M. Rivlin and J. M. Weiner, *Caring for the Disabled Elderly: Who Will Pay?* (Washington: Brookings Institution, 1988). R. L. Associates, *The American Public Views Long-Term Care.*

87. E. Hing, E. Sekscenski, and G. Strahan, *The National Nursing Home Survey,* 1985 Summary for the United States, Vital and Health Statistics, Public Health Service, Series 13, No. 97, DHHS Pub. No. (PHS) 89-1758 (Washington: GPO, 1987).

88. Institute of Medicine, *Improving The Quality of Care in Nursing Homes* (Washington: National Academy Press, 1986).

89. M. P. LaPlante, *Data on Disability from the National Health Interview Survey, 1983-85, Prepared for the National Institute on Disability and Rehabilitation Research* (Washington: U.S. Department of Education, 1988).

90. E. Hing et al., *The National Nursing Home Survey.*

91. U.S. Bipartisan Commission on Comprehensive Health Care, *A Call for Action.* Rivlin and Weiner, *Caring for the Disabled Elderly: Who Will Pay?*

92. Kane and Kane, *A Will and a Way.*

93. D. Justice, *State Long-Term Care Reform: Development of Community Care Systems in Six States* (Washington: National Governors' Association, 1988).

94. R. J. Newcomer, C. Harrington, A. Friedlob et al., *Evaluation of the Social Health Maintenance Organization Demonstration* (Washington: DHHS, Health Care Financing Administration, Pub. No. 03283, 1989); R.T. Zawadski, "The Long-Term Care Demonstration Projects: What They Are and Why They Come into Being," *Home Health Care Services Quarterly* 4 (1983).

95. L. J. Campbell and K. D. Cole, "Geriatric Assessment Teams," *Clinics in Geriatric Medicine* 3:1 (1987), 99-117.

96. GAO, *Report to the Chairman: Subcommittee on Health and Long-Term Care, Select Committee on Aging* (Washington: GAO, 1987).

97. DHHS, Division of Nursing, 1988 National Sample Survey of Registered Nurses, unpublished data; D. Himmelstein and S. Woolhandler, "Who Cares for the Caregivers? Lack of Health Insurance Among Health and Insurance Personnel," *JAMA* 266 (1991), 399-401.

98. William H. Barker, *Adding Life to Years: Organized Geriatric Services in Great Britain and Implications for the United States* (Baltimore: Johns Hopkins University Press, 1987).

99. Roger Feldman and Michael A. Morissey, "Health Economics: A Report on the Field," *Journal of Health, Politics and Law* 15 (1990), 627.

100. Blendon, "Three Systems."

101. David Corn, "Big Players vs. Single Payer," *The Nation,* April 26, 1993.

102. S. Woolhandler and D. Himmelstein, "Galloping Toward Oligopoly: Giant HMO 'A' or Giant HMO 'B'," *The Nation,* September 19, 1994.

103. Suzanne Gordon and Judith Shindul-Rothschild, "The Managed Care Scam," *The Nation,* May 16, 1994.

104. For a detailed discussion of the politics leading to the enactment of the British National Health Service Act, see Michael Foot, *Aneurin Bevan: A Biography* (London: Davis-Poynter Ltd., 1973), pp. 101-218, and John Campbell, *Aneurin Bevan and the Mirage of British Socialism* (New York: Norton, 1987), pp. 165-85.

105. Woolhandler and Himmelstein, *Chartbook,* p. 148; John Colombotas and Corinne Kirchner, *Physicians and Social Change* (New York: Oxford University Press, 1986).

Afterword

The publishers of *The Rational Option* invited Hillary Rodham Clinton to participate in a serious intellectual exchange with the authors of this work. In light of the failure of the 103rd Congress to enact any health care reform, the time was considered ripe for serious reflection and discussion among those who have advocated universal coverage, albeit by different means. Mrs. Clinton's Special Assistant, Jennifer Klein, called our office on several occasions indicating Mrs. Clinton's deep interest in the manuscript and pressed us to send the completed footnotes as quickly as possible. A thoughtful response to Woolhandler, Himmelstein, and Canham-Clyne was not ruled out and a final decision was left pending. However, over several months a formal reply did not materialize. Finally, as this work was going to press we were informed by the White House that Mrs. Clinton would "not be writing a reply to Himmelstein and Woolhandler." A proposal for reform as significant as Medicare or Social Security and backed by the single largest block of Congressional representatives was not deemed worthy of a thoughtful critique.

We are not interested in avoiding discussion about the contents of this book. Indeed, we seek to enlarge the circle of debate. If the courage can one day be found to face, rather than avoid, the underlying thesis presented in *The Rational Option,* then our door will remain open to an intelligent and lucid dialogue in a future edition. A serious reply to the critique offered here of the conceptual notions and tactics adopted by the Clinton Administration was not only timely but crucial to understanding the political debacle which overcame the Clinton effort at reform. Undoubtedly, at this juncture it would have required both courage and honest reflection to engage in such a debate. If, in fact, the single-payer system, is not the most rational option, then let us hear a clear and reasoned argument against it. We doubt it can be made in serious intellectual terms. And we think this is precisely why proponents of the Clinton schema prefer instead to argue with those who essentially favor the *status quo* and oppose any reform.

In February 1993 in a discussion between Dr. David Himmelstein and Hillary Clinton the distinction between what is rational and what (at least then) appeared to be politically expedient was set out in stark terms. Although this encounter has been mentioned in passing, the full description of the Himmelstein–Clinton exchange reported in *The Nation* is worth citing in detail.

> *"Senators tell me this," notes Senator Paul Wellstone, who has introduced a single-payer bill. "They say, 'look your bill is [the] most desirable, but the organized special interest groups can't accept it. It can't pass. You bump up against the insurance industry, the pharmaceutical companies, and others. And we've got to pass something.'"*
>
> *In Washington all policy is politics. That's no secret. Those advocating a revolutionary reform—one that would eviscerate one of the American people's least favorite industries, the insurance trade—are being told to get real, to work within the borders. The word comes from on high. Several national advocates of a single*

payer system, including Dr. David Himmelstein of Physicians for a National Health Program, sat down with Hillary Clinton in February. She listened attentively, asked smart questions—how would such a system encourage more health providers to perform primary care rather than specialize?—but she gave no indication their presentations would make a dent in her plan, some form of managed competition in which the health care delivery system is organized into large purchasing cooperatives likely to be dominated by insurance companies.

It was evident Hillary is thinking a lot about politics. Can you realistically tell me, she asked, that there are any big powers that support single-payer and that can take on the insurance industry's lobbying and advertising budget? "I said, 'about 70% of the people in the U.S. favor something like a single-payer system,'" Himmelstein recalls. "'With presidential leadership that can be an overwhelming force.' She said, 'David, tell me something interesting.'" *

In this work, David Himmelstein and his colleagues not only say something interesting, but set their argument within a principled framework unfettered by political expediency. In their view, realistic solutions can only be achieved when they are part of a rational course of action. When reforms represent clear and unambiguous principles, it also becomes possible to mobilize public opinion into a powerful force. In fact, what is genuinely interesting is that the Clinton Administration totally failed to effectively "take on the insurance industry's lobbying and advertising budget" because it alienated its own political base with abject compromises.

Many hold that if the Clinton Administration had embraced the single-payer option early on, it would have been

---

*David Corn, "Healthcare Reform: Big Players vs. Single Payer," *The Nation*, April 26, 1993.

in a position to mobilize a vast constituency among trade unionists, the elderly, medical professionals, the progressive intellectual community, and broad sections of the so-called middle class. A series of well-organized marches on Washington could have brought hundreds of thousands of supporters to the capital demanding passage of legislation which directly affected the security and health of their families. Congress could have been compelled to feel the pressure. Indeed, it was the only *realistic* way to counter the purchasing power of Washington lobbyists and the well-financed interests that stood behind them. But hubris preceded defeat. Instead, Americans were presented with a set of expedient compromises which could only increase the destructive power of the insurance industry over the nation's health care system. It was simply not a viable political platform around which a popular base could be organized.

The path toward a more rational society where unnecessary suffering and economic waste are minimized has always been resisted by those forces which Thorstein Veblen once called the "vested interests." It is these interests which have succeeded in keeping tens of millions of American citizens without adequate medical coverage. Anchored in the private insurance industry, the opponents of reform waged a propaganda war in 1993–94 for a paltry $50 million. For another $46 million in "contributions" they called in their political markers on key Congressional Committees where Republicans and Democrats alike colluded to insure that any coherent legislation would not be put to a vote by the 103rd Congress. By making a few wise investments, the insurance industry tied Congress neatly into knots and held on to forty billion dollars a year in profits and overhead.

The Clinton Administration came to power with a promise to carry out one of the most significant social reforms since the Roosevelt Administration created Social Security. For those who favored the establishment of a universal health care system there were two possible roads to follow. The first path, advocated by the authors of *The Rational Option,* was clear: a single-payer option that would abolish the health insurance industry. Single-payer advocates were implacably opposed to any compromise with those who, for the sake of pecuniary gain, had denied Americans, for more than two generations, a national health program equivalent to what every other advanced industrial state possessed. In their view, an effective political strategy had to confront such lobbies head on and systematically organize their political defeat. In Europe and in Canada, the social democratic parties succeeded in bringing universal health care to their societies because they clearly understood this elementary requirement.

The other option was compromise, the dead-end path taken by the Clintons. As this work demonstrates, the Clinton Administration sought to accommodate its potential enemy by mediating its reform through the private insurance industry. Early on they issued guarantees as "New Democrats" that no part of the industry would be "socialized" as had been done in Western Europe and Canada, or in the United States under the New Deal legislation establishing Social Security. Believing they could dine at the same table with wolves, the Clintons soon discovered that their reform proposals had been eaten alive by the guests.

At her Wellesley College graduation, Hillary Clinton spoke in reply to the commencement speaker, Senator Edward Brooke, who had disparaged student involvement in the anti-war movement. She replied sharply. In her own speech, she noted the principles and idealism which informed the actions taken by critics of the Vietnam War and referred to the slogan which had appeared on the walls of the Sorbonne during 1968: *"Demand the impossible. Settle for nothing less."* A quarter century later such ill-placed utopian notions would certainly not inform the tactics of the Clinton health care reform effort. Instead, other more Faustian strategies would be pursued.

As this work makes clear, quality universal coverage will not be achieved by compromise with the adversaries of reform. The Clinton effort is part of history. The attempt to buy off the opposition to substantive reform has failed. It must now be superseded by a sober approach which is demonstrably rational and sets as its task the unconditional political defeat of those interests which would deny Americans a comprehensive and humane medical system.

The Rational Option is a book for the future. As publishers, we believe in being fair. Our doors remain open to a critical and serious dialogue. If Hillary Clinton can explain why the *common sense* underlying the thesis presented in these pages is irrational, then we are open to including her critique in a future printing. Perhaps, Mrs. Clinton might, even now, be able to tell us "something interesting."

LAWRENCE LIFSCHULTZ
Editorial Committee

Resources

For additional information on how to participate in the establishment of a National Health Program of universal health care based on a single-payer model contact the organizations listed below.

PHYSICIANS FOR A NATIONAL HEALTH PROGRAM
332 South Michigan Avenue, Suite 500
Chicago, Illinois 60604
Tel: 312-554-0382
Fax: 312-554-0383

PUBLIC CITIZEN HEALTH RESEARCH GROUP
2000 P Street, N.W.
Washington, D.C. 20036
Tel: 202-546-4996

UNIVERSAL HEALTH CARE ACTION NETWORK
2800 Euclid Avenue, Suite 520
Cleveland, Ohio 44115
Tel: 216-241-8422

NURSES FOR NATIONAL HEALTH CARE
15 South Wright
Naperville, Illinois 60540
Tel: 708-983-0886

The authors and publishers of *The Rational Option* will be contributing a portion of the sales to Physicians for a National

Health Program and other public interest organizations campaigning on behalf of a single-payer program. Non-profit organizations and groups at the national and local level involved in public education on behalf of a National Health Program may apply to the publisher for special discounts.

The Authors

JOHN CANHAM-CLYNE is a Washington journalist who has written and reported for *The Progressive, World Policy Journal, Pacifica Radio,* and *In These Times.*

DR. STEFFIE WOOLHANDLER and DR. DAVID HIMMELSTEIN are on the staff of the Cambridge Hospital and are Associate Professors at Harvard Medical School. They are founding members of Physicians for a National Health Program, which is committed to the establishment of a single-payer system of national health insurance.

PAUL WELLSTONE is U.S. Senator from Minnesota. He is the leading proponent in the U.S. Senate of a National Health Program based on a single-payer system.